LIVING WITH A CLEAR CONSCIENCE

D0963795

The Living as a Christian Series:

Basic Christian Maturity

Growing in Faith
  Steve Clark
Knowing God's Will
  Steve Clark
Decision to Love
  Ken Wilson
God First
  Ken Wilson
Sons and Daughters of God
  Ken Wilson

Overcoming Obstacles to Christian Living

How to Repair the Wrong You've Done
  Ken Wilson
Getting Free
  Bert Ghezzi

The Emotions

The Angry Christian
  Bert Ghezzi
The Self-Image of a Christian
  Mark Kinzer
Living with a Clear Conscience
  Mark Kinzer

Christian Character

Strength under Control
  John Keating
*How to Become the Person You
  Were Meant to Be*
  Peter Williamson

**Bert Ghezzi and Peter Williamson
General Editors**

Living with a Clear Conscience

A Christian Strategy for Overcoming Guilt and Self-Condemnation

Mark Kinzer

SERVANT BOOKS
Ann Arbor, Michigan

Copyright © 1982 by Mark Kinzer
All rights reserved.

Published by Servant Books
P.O. Box 8617
Ann Arbor, Michigan 48107

Cover Photo © Ed Cooper Enterprises
Book Design by John B. Leidy

Scripture quotations are taken from the Revised
Standard Version of the Bible, copyrighted 1946, 1952
© 1971, 1973. Where portions of the scripture
quotations appear in italics, the emphasis has been
added by the author.

Printed in the United States of America.
ISBN 0-89283-115-4

Contents

Living as a Christian

IN HUMAN TERMS, it is not easy to decide to follow Jesus Christ and to live our lives as Christians. Jesus requires that we surrender our selves to him, relinquish our aspirations for our lives, and submit our will to God. Men and women have never been able to do this easily; if we could, we wouldn't need a savior.

Once we accept the invitation and decide to follow Jesus, a new set of obstacles and problems asserts itself. We find that we are often ignorant about what God wants of us as his sons and daughters. For example, what does it mean practically to obey the first commandment—to love God with our whole mind, heart, and strength? How can we know God's will? How do we love people we don't like? How does being a Christian affect what we do with our time and money? What does it mean "to turn the other cheek"? In these areas—and many others—it is not easy to understand exactly what God wants.

Even when we do know what God wants, it can be quite difficult to apply his teaching to our daily lives. Questions abound. How do we find time to pray regularly? How do we repair a relationship with someone we have wronged or who has wronged us? How do we andle unruly emotional reactions? These are examples of perplexing questions about the application of Christian teaching to our daily lives.

Furthermore, we soon discover that Christians have enemies—the devil outside and the flesh within. Satan tempts us to sin; our inner urges welcome the temptation, and we find our will to resist steadily eroding.

Finally, we must overcome the world. We are living in an environment that is hostile toward what Christians believe and how they live, and friendly toward those who believe and do the opposite. The world in which we live works on our Christian resolve in many subtle ways. How much easier it is to think and act like those around us! How do we persevere?

There is a two-fold answer to these questions: To live successfully as Christians, we need both grace and wisdom. Both are freely available from the Lord to those who seek him.

As Christians we live by grace. The very life of God works in us as we try to understand God's teaching, apply it to our lives, and overcome the forces that would turn us aside from our chosen path. We always need grace, and grace is always there. The Lord is with us always, and the supply of his grace is inexhaustible.

Yet grace works with wisdom. Christians must *learn* a great deal about how to live according to God's will. We must study God's word in scripture, listen to Christian teaching, and reflect on our own experience and the experience of others. Many Christians today lack this kind of wisdom. This is the need which the *Living as a Christian* series is designed to meet.

The book you are reading is part of a series of books intended to help Christians apply the teaching of scripture to their lives. The authors of *Living as a Christian* books are pastoral leaders who have given this teaching in programs of Christian formation in various Christian communities. The teaching has stood the test of time. It has already helped many people grow as faithful servants of the Lord. We decided it was time to make this teaching available in book form.

All the *Living as a Christian* books seek to meet the following criteria:

- **Biblical.** The teaching is rooted in scripture. The authors and editors maintain that scripture is the word of God, and that it ought to determine what Christians believe and how they live.

- **Practical.** The purpose of the series is to offer down-to-earth advice about living as a Christian.

- **Relevant.** The teaching is aimed at the needs we encounter in our daily lives—at home, in school, on the job, in our day-to-day relationships.

- **Brief and Readable.** We have designed the series for busy people from a wide variety of backgrounds. Each of the authors presents profound Christian truths as simply and clearly as possible, and illustrates those truths by examples drawn from personal experience.

- **Integrated.** The books in the series comprise a unified curriculum on Christian living. They do not present differing views, but rather they take a consistent approach.

The format of the series makes it suitable for both individual and group use. The books in *Living as a Christian* can be used in such group settings as Sunday school classes, adult education programs, prayer groups, classes for teenagers, women's groups, and as a supplement to Bible study.

The *Living as a Christian* series is divided into several sets of books, each devoted to a different aspect of Christian living. These sets include books on Christian maturity, emotions in the Christian life, the fruit of the Holy Spirit, Christian personal relationships, Christian service, and, very likely, on other topics as well.

This book, *Living with a Clear Conscience*, is part of a set covering the emotions in the Christian life. The nature of modern society forces us to be more concerned about our emotions than our Christian ancestors had to be. Not that they were un-emotional. Ironically, they were more expressive of their emotions than most of us are. But nowadays we look at our emotions differently, and the instability of relationships and pressures of modern life introduce some new problems. *Living with a Clear Conscience* and other books in this set present a practical scripturally based strategy for emotional health.

The editors dedicate the *Living as a Christian* series to Christian men and women everywhere who have counted the cost and decided to follow Jesus Christ as his disciples.

Bert Ghezzi and Peter Williamson
General Editors

Preface

Who shall bring any charge against God's elect? It is God who justifies; who is to condemn? Is it Christ Jesus, who died, yes, who was raised from the dead, who is at the right hand of God, who indeed intercedes for us? (Rom 8:33-34)

Paul's questions in this passage are merely rhetorical. He assumes that the answers are obvious. However, many Christians today give answers that Paul would not have expected. "Maybe you're right, Paul, about God the Father and the Lord Jesus—perhaps they don't condemn me (though I am not fully convinced). But there is someone else who brings a charge against me and condemns me—my conscience." Many Christians today live their lives under the tyranny of a merciless accuser and judge—their own distorted evaluation of themselves.

Self-condemnation is a problem. The proliferation of therapies designed to promote mental health is one indicator of the extent of the problem. Most of these therapies seek to relieve irrational feelings of guilt and self-hatred. Although some of them employ theories and techniques of questionable value, they do respond to a genuine need among modern people.

It is surprising to note the sheer variety of people who experience a problem with self-condemnation. Some of those who suffer from this problem have committed serious wrongdoing at some point in their lives; their self-condemnation builds on a foundation of objective guilt. However, many others are plagued by accusing thoughts, even though they have never committed a serious offense. Their overscrupulous moral convictions force them to struggle with self-condemnation. I have known self-condemned people who are shy, mild, and self-effacing, and I have known others who are bitter, resentful, and intolerant. The problem is manifested in different ways in different people, but the basic problem is the same—a nagging, persistent sense of moral unworthiness.

Most people who suffer from self-condemnation also have a more general problem with a poor self-image. At root, they doubt their essential worth as human beings. If their problem is extreme, they think themselves unloveable and unloved. A basic problem with a poor self-image and self-condemnation will manifest itself in a number of unfortunate behavior patterns: depression, self-pity, introspection, defensiveness, and the inability to receive praise and encouragement. One cannot always trace these patterns to a poor self-image, but it is often possible to do so. A poor self-image and a problem with self-condemnation not only make life uncomfortable; they also interfere with serving God and neighbor in the full fruitfulness of the Holy Spirit.[1]

Though one can view self-condemnation solely as a self-image problem, it has its own unique complications that arise from the spiritual reality of sin and guilt. When I am feeling worthless, I can readily speak the truth to myself: "You have been created and redeemed by the Lord of the universe, who has made you his special treasure and the apple of his eye. And you have the audacity to question your value?" However, when I am feeling self-condemned I cannot always exonerate myself: "You did nothing wrong. You are not guilty." Sometimes this is true, but not always. Thus, in order to deal properly with the emotional problem of self-condemnation, one must know how to approach wrongdoing and genuine objective guilt.

Like the more general problem of low self-esteem, self-condemnation afflicts many people in our society, Christian and otherwise. This, combined with the fact that self-condemnation is connected to important revealed truths concerning sin and guilt, makes it an important topic for modern Christians to understand properly.

Misunderstandings

The modern problem with self-condemnation is aggravated by Christian and secular misunderstandings about wrongdoing and repentance. Christians often confuse repentance and remorse with self-condemnation. Many Christians believe they are being virtuous by insisting on their moral worthlessness and indulging their feelings of guilt and inadequacy. This misunderstanding makes them more susceptible to an emotional problem of self-condemnation and aggravates problems that already exist.[2]

A certain false but widely accepted secular notion also increases problems with self-condemnation—the notion that firm moral norms undermine mental health and limit human happiness. Many people in our society seek freedom from feelings of guilt by pretending that objective guilt does not exist or that what most people in the past have called "guilt" is not the genuine article. For example, many people would hold that any type of sexual behavior between consenting adults is morally acceptable.

A lax approach to morality does not really help people overcome problems with self-condemnation. Instead, it makes them more subject to the emotional approval and disapproval of others, and thereby increases their feelings of insecurity and moral unworthiness.

The Goal

A major goal of this little book is to provide greater understanding of wrongdoing, guilt, repentance, remorse, and forgiveness—and to correct some of the above-stated misunderstandings along the way. However, an even more prominent goal is to offer practical teaching about how to overcome self-condemnation.

The first set of chapters discusses wrongdoing and repentance. As Christians, we must begin dealing with self-condemnation by squarely facing the reality of objective guilt. The second set of chapters describes some common misconceptions among Christians, misconceptions that increase problems with self-condemnation. These chapters attempt to draw a more accurate picture of the Christian teaching in the area of righteousness, repentance, and remorse. The final set of chapters offers practical advice for overcoming special problems with self-condemnation. Taken all together, I hope that this treatment of the problem will enable us to grow in the righteousness and freedom that belongs to us in Christ Jesus.

ONE

Wrongdoing, Guilt, and Righteousness

SELF-CONDEMNATION IS something that both Christians and non-Christians experience. What does a Christian approach to the topic have to offer that a secular approach does not?

Most secular counselors—psychologists and social workers—simply look at the emotional problem itself. They fail to penetrate deeper, to the roots of our troubled human condition. A Christian perspective, on the other hand, cannot afford to ignore the moral dimensions of the topic. Christians acknowledge that there is an objective standard of right and wrong. As Paul says, "All have sinned and fall short of the glory of God" (Rom 3:23). This is precisely where the Christian teaching on self-condemnation must begin.

The Secular Solution

A man walked into a medical clinic, his arm bleeding profusely. The examining physician gave him an injection to relieve his pain and then sent him home without cleaning the wound or stopping the bleeding. The man lost much blood and his wound became badly infected. He soon died a painless death.

This little parable illustrates the approach to self-condemnation and guilt taken by many modern people. Rather than treating the wound— the objective guilt that follows our wrongdoing— many focus merely on relieving the pain—our subjective feelings of guilt. In both cases the sensation of pain is not really the ultimate evil. Physical pain serves an essential function in the human body; it tells us that something is amiss with one of our members. Similarly, feelings of guilt are sometimes only signs pointing to an objective disorder demanding immediate attention. Just as it is possible to relieve all physical pain and die a speedy but comfortable death, so it is possible to remove all traces of subjective guilt and still forfeit one's soul.

The modern secular analysis of guilt usually rests on the following three fundamental propositions:

1. *Guilt is a subjective feeling, not an objective state.* One author states clearly: "Let us tentatively define guilt as a feeling that we have done or felt something unacceptable to someone."[3] Guilt, then, is merely a feeling. This definition allows one to examine the problem of self-condemnation without reference to concepts of right and wrong. To help a person overcome

self-condemnation one needn't inquire into their conduct. The real focus is on internal balance. If a person can only learn to gain control of their unruly emotions, they will no longer have a problem with guilt.

2. *Guilt originates in a child's experience of parental disapproval.* The same author also makes this point: "I believe all guilt originates from the fear a parent will harm us for what we do. This may even include our thoughts since many parents attempt to control their children's minds."[4] According to this view, not only do guilt *problems* have their roots in early childhood experiences, but *all* guilt has a similar psychological origin.

3. *Guilt problems stem from parental tyranny during childhood years and submission to emotional manipulation as an adult.* We feel guilty when we don't meet other people's expectations of us. Others know they can control our behavior by showing emotional disapproval, which induces guilt. If we are especially susceptible to this manipulation as a result of childhood experiences, we will certainly develop a guilt problem.

Thus, the secular approach manages to probe the nature and source of self-condemnation without using such moral terms as *right*, *wrong*, *should*, *ought*, *conscience*, *law*, or *obligation*.

Based on such an analysis, secular experts offer

a prescription for removing guilt feelings. Of course advice varies from expert to expert, but most of them agree on the following three counsels:

1. *"You are not doing anything wrong."* Innocence is here based not on a sound moral evaluation of conduct, but instead on removing whole categories of human behavior from the sphere of moral judgment. For example, "Your guilt feelings about committing incest are quite irrational. You are simply responding to the emotional pressure of your society. Sexual relations in private between consenting individuals are not morally objectionable." In psychological jargon, this technique for removing guilt is called "weakening the superego."

2. *"Your guilt problem is actually a result of early life experiences hidden elusively in the depth of your unconscious, and you must deal with the problem by getting to its source."* Thus, you feel guilty, not because you behaved inconsiderately towards your spouse, but because of an unresolved fear of your father's disapproval. If you want to banish today's guilt, you must first unearth those buried memories from yesterday.

3. *"Stop yielding to emotional blackmail."* Your guilt results from consistently allowing your behavior to be determined by everyone else's expectations. If you want to break free from bondage to guilt, then you must learn to

disregard what others want so that you can assert your own independent judgment. Don't let yourself be manipulated by others' emotional disapproval.

The secular perspective either denies or ignores the reality of objective guilt. Guilt is treated as merely another emotional disorder with no relation to an objective standard of behavior.

As Christians, we may be tempted to ridicule and dismiss all that these secular views assert. However, if we did so, we would be making a mistake. Secular approaches to guilt actually offer some helpful insights. That's why they're so popular. The following three assertions, drawn and adapted from these secular views, are true and helpful:

1. Many people who experience an irrational emotional problem with self-condemnation have committed no significant objective wrongdoing. Their problem is emotional, not moral.

2. Poor family relationships in childhood can make a person particularly susceptible to irrational emotional problems with self-condemnation.

3. Many people in our society use guilt to manipulate others. Such use of emotional pressure, usually indirect and unconscious, adds to a problem with irrational self-condemnation.

All these assertions provide valuable insights into the problem of self-condemnation. In the following chapters we will have greater opportunity to expand on them and apply them.

Even so, these secular analyses are unsound at their foundation. If Christianity is true, if scripture is reliable, if a righteous and holy God exists and rules over all, then it is impossible to dismiss the reality of objective moral norms. In fact, these norms are engraved on the very structure of the universe and on the structure of human nature. A Christian cannot consider the topic of guilt feelings without also studying its relationship to objective guilt.

Guilt and Guilt Feelings

Our society's loss of a sense of objective guilt is evident in the very usage of the word. The older understanding of guilt viewed it as "the fact of having committed a breach of conduct, especially violating law and involving a penalty" (first definition, *Webster's Seventh New Collegiate Dictionary*). One was guilty if one had transgressed an objective legal standard. But consider the newer definition: "a feeling of culpability for offenses" (second definition). Guilt is becoming an internal, subjective, emotional state rather than an objective fact.

Both scripture and traditional Christian teaching presume that there is such a thing as objective guilt. This is strikingly illustrated in the Old Testament book of Leviticus. In some passages of

Leviticus the word translated *guilt* applies particularly to unintentional and unknown sins, largely of a ritual nature:

> "If the whole congregation of Israel commits a sin unwittingly and the thing is hidden from the eyes of the assembly, and they do any of the things which the Lord has commanded not to be done *and are guilty*; when the sin which they have committed becomes known, the assembly shall offer a young bull for a sin offering and bring it before the tent of meeting." (Lev 4:13-14; see also Lev 4:22-24; 27-28; 5:1-2; 6:1-7)

What does scripture mean by *guilt*? This passage states it succinctly: If we "do any of the things which the Lord has commanded not to be done," then we "are guilty." According to Leviticus, objective guilt exists as soon as the offense has been committed, even if the guilty party does not know about the offense until later. Scripture presents guilt as an objective condition that follows upon the violation of God's commandments, rather than as an internal, subjective, emotional state.

To illustrate the contrast between guilt and guilt feelings, let us look for a moment at King David's adulterous relationship with Bathsheba and his murder of Uriah, Bathsheba's husband. This is the darkest incident in David's life. As we see in 2 Samuel 11, he yields first to his physical desire for Bathsheba. A problem arises—

Bathsheba conceives a child. Since her husband is away on a military campaign, he will know that the child does not belong to him. Therefore, David summons Uriah to his palace and tries to send him home so that he will have sexual relations with his wife. Uriah refuses out of loyalty to his general and fellow soldiers: "The ark and Israel and Judah dwell in booths; and my lord Joab and the servants of my lord are camping in the open field; shall I then go to my house, to eat and to drink, and to lie with my wife? As you live, and as your soul lives, I will not do this thing" (2 Sam 11:11).

Frustrated by Uriah's virtue, David sends a message to Joab, his general on the field of battle: "Set Uriah in the forefront of the hardest fighting, and then draw back from him, that he may be struck down, and die." Once the deed is done, David quickly proceeds to marry Bathsheba.

This chapter ends with a simple statement of God's view on the matter: "The thing that David had done displeased the Lord." David is guilty of grave sin. He has coveted his neighbor's wife, committed adultery with her, and murdered her husband—a man who was fiercely loyal to the king's own cause. He has taken advantage of the throne given him by the Lord to cruelly exploit a loyal subject. David stands guilty in the sight of God.

Yet, scripture gives no sign that David's conscience troubled him. He may have felt guilty or he may not have. We don't know. Regardless of how he felt, he *is* guilty, and the Lord makes that clear to him by sending the prophet Nathan with a parable designed to bring him to repentance. Nathan speaks of an unjust act committed by a rich man against a poor man. David responds with great anger, "The man who has done this deserves to die." Nathan then rejoins with the crushing words, "You are the man," and prophesies the Lord's punishment on David's house for his wicked deed. David immediately acknowledges his sin and sincerely repents. Still, the child born of adultery must die, for David's sin must be punished. For "by this deed you have utterly scorned the Lord."

When did David become guilty? According to the modern view, he was not guilty until Nathan had persuaded him to repent. Only then did he begin to feel guilty. This is the subjective view of guilt. But according to the biblical view, David was guilty the moment he sinned. In scripture and in Christian teaching, guilt is not simply an emotional state; it is an objective condition resulting from the violation of God's commands.

To point out the distinction between guilt and guilt feelings is not to imply that irrational feelings of guilt are insignificant and unworthy of discussion. In fact, the purpose of this book is to provide help in overcoming such feelings. Many of us have problems with irrational and destructive feelings of guilt that cripple us emotionally. We need to learn how to handle them, and we need to experience the liberating power of God's grace. But if we *are* guilty, if we have done something wrong in God's sight, we cannot simply soothe our tormented feelings of guilt. The fundamental problem, at the root of the human spiritual condition, is objective guilt, not subjective guilt. Wrongdoing must be dealt with before one can sort out an emotional guilt problem.

If we are to live the Christian life, we must take objective guilt seriously. We cannot have a right relationship with God if we refuse to walk in righteousness and to repair wrongdoing. It is better to live righteously and suffer some measure of emotional turmoil than to be liberated from every feeling of guilt and yet live in a way that displeases the Lord.

Fortunately, these are not the alternatives set before us. If we approach objective guilt seriously and with wisdom, we will also be freed from irrational feelings of guilt. Conversely, the denial of objective standards of guilt does not really eliminate problems with self-condemnation. The absence of objective standards only subjects people more fully to the tyranny of others' emotional approval and disapproval.

The first piece of advice for handling guilt feelings is also the easiest to understand: If you don't want to *feel* guilty, don't *be* guilty. This is not all that needs to be said on the topic, but it is the first thing to be said.

Loving Righteousness

God has clearly revealed the standards by which he judges human behavior. When we act according to these standards, we are behaving righteously; when we violate them, we are behaving unrighteously or sinfully. God's intention in creating us in his image and likeness and in re-creating us in Christ is to make us righteous men and women who obey him in everything.

The Lord wants a people who take joy in obeying his word. We are not only called to act righteously, but also to "hunger and thirst for righteousness" (Mt 5:6). In Psalm 11:7 we learn that "the Lord is righteous, he loves righteous deeds." And in Psalm 45:6-7 we read of the Messianic King, "Your royal scepter is a scepter of equity; you love righteousness and hate wickedness." We also should love righteousness and hate wickedness. Obedience to the law of God should not be a matter of dreary obligation for us, but a matter of joy and delight.

> Blessed is the man
>> who walks not in the counsel of the wicked,
> nor stands in the way of sinners,
>> nor sits in the seat of scoffers;
> but his delight is in the law of the Lord,
>> and on his law he meditates day and night.
>> (Ps 1:1-2)

If we love the Lord and rejoice in his salvation, then we should also love his commandments and desire to please him in everything.

The English word *righteousness* has lost its appeal for many of us in recent years. The word seems hard, cold, and impersonal, and is often associated with the term *self-righteousness*. In contrast, Christians of the past have delighted in the very word *righteousness* since it communicates something of the just order of God's eternal kingdom. If we rejoice to do God's will and long to see all of creation submitted to his authority, then it will not be difficult for us to "hunger and thirst for righteousness" and to delight in the very word itself.

God created us to live righteously before him, obeying his commandments and fulfilling his purposes. We read in the book of Genesis that Adam and Eve violated God's command not to eat from the tree of the knowledge of good and evil, and we also read of the penalty they suffered as a result of their disobedience: expulsion from the garden and the tree of life. The Apostle Paul sees Christ's great redemptive act of obedience—his giving of his life on the cross—as cancelling out the disobedience of Adam and Eve and inaugurating a new era of righteousness:

> Then as one man's trespass led to condemnation for all men, so one man's act of righteousness leads to acquittal and life for all men. For as by one man's disobedience many were made sinners, so by one man's obedience many will be made righteous. (Rom 5:18-19)

One of the main purposes of Jesus' mission was to restore righteousness to the earth. He lived his own life as an obedient son, demonstrating the true image and likeness of God, that the divine image of righteousness might be restored in us:

> Put off your old nature [or man—Adam] which belongs to your former manner of life and is corrupt through deceitful lusts, and be renewed in the spirit of your minds, and put on the new nature [or man—the second Adam], created after the likeness of God in true righteousness and holiness. (Eph 4:22-23)

Christ is the second Adam (1 Cor 15:47) whose gift of new life frees us from the bondage to disobedience that we inherited from the first Adam. He enables us to walk in true righteousness and holiness.

The Lord wants us to love righteousness and to see it as the purpose of Christ's redemptive act. However, he also wants us to recognize that we need his grace if we are to obey his commands. As the passage quoted above from Romans 5 states clearly, it is *Christ* who makes us righteous. We can live righteously only because we live in him and he lives in us. Paul makes this clear in his prayer for the Philippians:

> And it is my prayer that your love may abound more and more, with knowledge and all discernment, so that you may approve what is excellent, and may be pure and blameless for the day of Christ, filled with the fruits of righteousness

which come through Jesus Christ, to the glory
and praise of God. (Phil 1:9-11)

The fruits of righteousness come through a relationship with Jesus Christ, the Holy and Righteous One (Acts 3:14).

Many people think that righteousness and obedience must lead to a life that is dull, guilt-ridden, and joyless. Christianity is popularly associated with weak, introspective people, who grapple continuously with feelings of unworthiness and self-condemnation. Of course, some Christians do struggle with such feelings. However, their problem does not stem from an over-zealous dedication to righteousness, but instead from the same self-image problems that non-Christians experience. It is foolish and even dangerous to attempt to help someone overcome feelings of self-condemnation by eliminating or diluting their concern for righteousness.

In contrast to the modern view, the Bible teaches that righteousness leads to strength, life, and joy. This is especially clear in the Book of Psalms and the Book of Proverbs:

The righteous flourish like a palm tree,
and grow like a cedar of Lebanon. (Ps 92:12)

He who trusts in his riches shall wither,
but the righteous will flourish like a green
leaf. (Prv 11:28)

In the path of righteousness is life,
but the way of error leads to death.
(Prv 12:28)

He who pursues righteousness and kindness
will find life and honor. (Prv 21:21)

The hope of the righteous ends in gladness,
but the expectation of the wicked comes to
nought. (Prv 10:28)

An evil man is ensnared in his transgression
but a righteous man sings and rejoices.
(Prv 29:6)

Obedience to God is not only right and obligatory—
it is also the way we were created to live. We will
experience strength, joy, and fruitfulness when we
bend our necks to the yoke of righteousness.

In conclusion, we see that the modern secular
perspective on wrongdoing, guilt, and righteousness is badly distorted. We can learn some things
from secular attempts to remedy emotional
problems with self-condemnation, but we should
not accept a view that subjectivizes the concept of
guilt, making it a mere feeling unrelated to
objective moral standards. Nor should we accept a
view that undermines our love for righteousness.
Christian revelation clearly contradicts these
secular ideas. They are also inconsistent with
God's wisdom for overcoming problems with self-
condemnation. God wants his people both to love
righteousness and to live with a clear conscience,
and he will provide the power and the wisdom
required for the fulfillment of his purpose.

TWO

Repairing Wrongdoing

WHEN I WAS preparing for baptism many years ago, I learned that faith and baptism would enable me to put on Jesus Christ (Gal 3:27) and receive the power to conquer sin and live a life of righteousness. This teaching proved substantially true in experience. I soon found a new freedom to overcome wrong patterns of behavior. However, I also found that my sinful flesh had not totally thrown in the towel. Occasionally I would fall back into patterns of speech or thought that were part of the old man and not the new. In Christ, I was now living a basically righteous life, but I still needed some way of dealing with the wrong things I did.

My experience is certainly not unique. No matter how many years the Lord has worked with us to produce a proven Christian character, we still lapse and stumble and even fall. Our finite, human imperfection manifests itself frequently, and our stubborn, independent will resurfaces time and again. Often these lapses damage not only our relationship with the Lord but also our relationships with other people. In order to maintain a right relationship with the Lord and with others, we must learn how to repair the damage caused by our wrongdoing.

There are two main reasons why we should study the topic of repairing wrongdoing at this point. First, we must learn how to deal with the objective guilt that results from wrongdoing before we can proceed to discuss the emotional problem of self-condemnation. If I were a secular counselor with no belief in an objective right and wrong, I might turn immediately to a discussion of guilt feelings. But since I am a Christian pastor who believes that guilt is primarily an objective spiritual reality and only secondarily a psychological problem, it is necessary first to consider how to deal with real guilt that results from wrongdoing.

The second reason bears more directly on the problem that many of us experience with self-condemnation. The inability to repair wrongdoing often increases a sense of self-condemnation. For example, Sam yells at his wife Lois one morning for burning his toast and pestering him with questions while he is trying to read the sports section of the newspaper. Later in the morning, he realizes that he acted wrongly, but he does not know how to repair the wrong. He thus spends part of the day feeling self-condemned about what he has done and about his relationship with his wife. This behavior pattern is common to many of us—we act wrongly, we do not know how to repair the wrong, and thus we exact an emotional punishment from ourselves as a way of atoning for our misconduct.

Sam's problem is often further aggravated by Lois. Because she doesn't understand how to repair wrongdoing either, she is unable to confront her husband in a clear and straightforward manner. Instead, she expresses her resentment at her husband's morning insult by withdrawing her affection from him. She ignores her husband when he comes home from work, acknowledging his presence only by asking him to take out the trash. As they go to bed that night, she immediately turns away from him and pretends to sleep. In short, Lois increases Sam's emotional punishment by relating coldly and impersonally. Lois' reaction to her husband's wrongdoing only increases the likelihood that he will develop an emotional problem with self-condemnation.

Sam and Lois need a clear, straightforward method for confronting wrongdoing and becoming reconciled to each other. Sam should be able to go directly to Lois to repair the damaged relationship. He can repair what he has done wrong—he need not inflict an emotional beating upon himself. Lois should also be able to speak directly to her husband about the problem when he comes home from work, not penalizing him with the cold shoulder but correcting him in love.

Like them, we will be much better equipped to overcome an emotional problem with self-condemnation if we know how to repair wrongdoing in a direct, clear, and straightforward manner.

Repentance and Reconciliation

According to scripture, the way to repair wrong-doing is to repent and seek forgiveness. This applies to disruptions both in our relationship with God and in our relationships with other human beings. Reconciliation comes through repentance and forgiveness.

In the Old Testament, the Hebrew word for repentance literally means to turn or return or to change. Similarly, the Greek word for repentance in the New Testament means to change your mind. Both words indicate a resolution to forsake an old path and walk down a new one. The main word for forgiveness in the New Testament means to discharge, let go, or set free, and primarily derives from the realm of economics and law. To forgive someone means to release them from a debt that they owe you. This word was then applied by analogy to the debt incurred by sin. Thus Matthew's version of the Lord's Prayer states "forgive us our debts," meaning "release us and free us from the debt we owe you because of our sins." The two words *repentance* and *forgiveness* are often linked together in scripture to describe the process by which a disrupted relationship is restored. The offender resolves to change his ways, and then asks the offended party for forgiveness (see Acts 2:37-38). If the offended party responds by granting forgiveness (as Christians should), the end result is *reconciliation*—the establishment of a right relationship and peace between two parties who were formerly at odds with one another.

There are basically two types of repentance and forgiveness. The first type usually occurs at the beginning of our relationship with the Lord, when we turn from a life that is seriously at odds with God's commandments and begin leading a life submitted to God's will. This initial act of repentance is sometimes called *conversion*. When we convert, we are responding to God's gracious call to enter a new relationship with him in Jesus Christ. Our past relationship with God was seriously disrupted, but it is restored when we receive God's grace in Christ by faith and repentance. This type of repentance—which involves the restoration of a fundamentally disrupted relationship—can also occur when a Christian turns aside from the Lord for a period of time and falls into a life of serious wrongdoing.

This first type of repentance is what Jesus talks about in this passage from Luke's Gospel:

There were some present at that very time who told him of the Galileans whose blood Pilate had mingled with their sacrifices. And he answered them, "Do you think that these Galileans were worse sinners than all the other Galileans, because they suffered thus? I tell you, No; but unless you repent you will all likewise perish. Or those eighteen upon whom the tower in Siloam fell and killed them, do you think that they were worse offenders than all the others who dwelt in Jerusalem? I tell you, No; but unless you repent you will all likewise perish." (13:1-5)

Like John the Baptist, Jesus issues a general call to Israel to repent. What kind of repentance was he talking about? Consider his words, "But unless you repent you will all likewise perish." The people's relationship with God was fundamentally disrupted, and unless they were reconciled to God, they would die. Jesus was calling for a fundamental reorientation of their lives—a total turning from sin to righteousness.

Most Christians think of repentance primarily in terms of this first type—the restoration of a seriously ruptured relationship. However, a second type of repentance is extremely important if we are to live the Christian life successfully. This type of repentance involves the repair of less serious disruptions in our relationships. We could call it *daily repentance*. Daily repentance deals with the minor conflicts and disorders that arise in any relationship, even those relationships that are healthy and basically in good order. "Take heed to yourselves; if your brother sins, rebuke him, and if he repents, forgive him; and if he sins against you seven times in the day, and turns to you seven times, and says, 'I repent,' you must forgive him" (Lk 17:3-4). In this passage Jesus envisions a type of repentance and forgiveness that occurs frequently, even "seven times in the day" (a deliberate exaggeration for emphasis). When Jesus talks about repenting this frequently, he is probably not talking about our need to repent of such sins as adultery, robbery, or slander, but of sins like irritability, laziness, self-centeredness, irresponsibility, and the like.

Because most Christians think of repentance primarily in terms of conversion and because they misunderstand the actual meaning of repentance, they neglect the great practical value of repentance and forgiveness. Repentance is not reserved for just one or two major occasions in our life; nor is it something that only affects our relationship with God; nor is it merely an emotion or an attitude. Repentance is a practical tool given us by God for restoring damaged relationships. The damage may be serious or it may be slight, but it can always be repaired if we understand and apply the principles of repentance and forgiveness.

In the following pages I will briefly outline a practical approach to repentance and forgiveness which applies to both conversion and daily repentance, though our focus will be particularly on daily repentance.[5]

This approach involves four steps: (1) acknowledging wrongdoing, (2) renouncing wrongdoing, (3) asking forgiveness, and (4) making restitution. This approach applies both to our relationship with God and with other human beings. Let's look at each of these steps in order.

Step One: Acknowledging Wrongdoing

The first step of repentance is to acknowledge and honestly admit our wrongdoing. This is not an easy task. Our usual tendency is to make excuses, to rationalize our guilt, or to flatly deny that we have done anything wrong. We eagerly avoid the one thing that we need to do—take responsibility for our wrongdoing.

One reason why many of us fail to take responsibility for our wrongdoing is that we have adopted a blame-excuse approach to relationship problems. When we've done something wrong, we ask, "Am I to blame for this act I have just committed, or can the act be excused?" The following considerations may float through our minds: "Who could blame me for being so irritable? I hardly slept a wink last night and haven't had a thing to eat all day." "I've been under a lot of pressure lately. How can anyone expect me to keep it together?" "She was so obnoxious that I couldn't help telling her off." "My father and mother never disciplined me when I was young; I'm really not to blame." All of these factors may be relevant, and they may point out truly extenuating circumstances. Nonetheless, this blame-excuse model is the wrong approach for dealing with wrongdoing.

Another reason why many of us fail to take responsibility for our wrongdoing is that we place too much emphasis on our intentions. Instead of simply trying to ascertain whether we have *done* something that is objectively wrong, we probe our underlying motives to see if they were pure or impure. "Sure, I forgot to pick up Mr. Baker on the way to work, but I didn't do it on purpose."

"Sure, I spilled green paint all over Mary's new shoes, but I didn't mean to; it was an accident." "Well, you see, Professor Anderson, I meant to write that paper, but other things came up." Motives certainly do make a difference—our guilt is increased greatly if we do something from malice rather than from negligence. Nonetheless, our intention is not the only factor that determines whether we have done something wrong, something for which we should take responsibility.

What matters is not whether we should be blamed or excused for our action (though extenuating circumstances should be accounted for); or whether our intentions were good (though it is much better to have good intentions than evil ones); the point at issue concerns whether I have done something objectively wrong that has damaged a personal relationship with someone, either God or a human being. If so, then I need to take responsibility for my action, acknowledging it honestly, clearly, and straightforwardly.

Of course our actions may hurt someone even though they do not fall into the category of wrongdoing. Sometimes we have no control over circumstances and are forced to make the best of a bad situation. For example, you may fail to pick up Mrs. Baker for church because your car stalls out on the way. You may not be able to find a telephone to call her and explain the situation. In such an instance you haven't done anything wrong and should not acknowledge wrongdoing, even though you could genuinely express your regret by calling her as soon as you are able.

Curiously, those who feel most guilty and experience the most self-condemnation often have the most difficulty acknowledging their wrongdoing. I know one young woman who has a poor self-image and experiences a constant sense of moral unworthiness. Though she feels bad about things she has done in the past and though she believes that she is an evil person, she finds it very hard to acknowledge specific wrongdoing after she commits it. Instead, she blames it on other people and institutions and the difficult circumstances she faces. Her dissatisfaction with herself thus expresses itself in dissatisfaction with other people and with her circumstances. But because she is unable to acknowledge her wrongdoing, her relationships with other people suffer, and her self-hatred and self-pity only increase.

When we acknowledge our wrongdoing, we should be clear, specific, and concrete. It's not enough simply to confess our basic sinfulness— we must also confess our particular sins. Whenever I find myself feeling a vague sense of self-condemnation, I try to determine whether I've done something wrong recently that I've failed to repair. With some regularity I discover some unacknowledged and unrepaired wrongdoing. The Lord doesn't want us to confess our feelings of guilt; instead, he wants us to acknowledge and confess to him the specific things that we have done wrong and that have displeased him.

In Psalm 32, David describes the pain of

harboring wrongdoing and the freedom that comes from honest confession:

> When I declared not my sin, my body wasted
> away
>   through my groaning all day long.
> For day and night thy hand was heavy upon me;
>   my strength was dried up as by the heat of
>   summer.
> I acknowledged my sin to thee,
>   and I did not hide my iniquity;
> I said, "I will confess my transgressions to the
>   Lord";
>   then thou didst forgive the guilt of my sin.
>
> (Ps 32:3-5)

Forgiveness and reconciliation begin when we honestly acknowledge our wrongdoing.

Step Two: Renouncing Wrongdoing

As we saw earlier, the word for repentance in Greek and Hebrew literally means to turn or to change your mind. Thus, to repent of wrongdoing means to turn aside from it—by renouncing it, expressing sorrow for it, and resolving to not do it again.

Two obstacles arise here. First, we sometimes refuse to renounce wrongdoing because we simply do not want to. We aren't really sorry for what we've done. If given the opportunity, we would probably do the same thing again. I knew one man who was always late for everything—work, dinner, church, you name it. He would always apologize in a sincere manner and express his sorrow for making you wait. But you knew that he would be late again the next time. Finally he realized that his repentance was hollow, and he decided not only to apologize but to change. From then on he was rarely ever late. His repentance became genuine when he made a firm resolution to behave differently.

The second obstacle is a more challenging one. Some of us fail to renounce wrongdoing because we lack confidence in our ability to change. We want to turn away from a particular wrong act, but we seem to lack the power and strength to do so. Perhaps we have tried with little success to overcome an area of weakness that has persisted over a period of years. It has tenaciously resisted our attempts to change. Mary has always been impatient with her children, and she knows she cannot change; Harold has always been critical of his father, and he knows he cannot change; Michael has been an alcoholic for years, and he knows he cannot change.

This is not only a confidence problem—it is also a faith problem. Remember Paul's words to the Corinthians, "God is faithful, and he will not let you be tempted beyond your strength, but with the temptation will also provide the way of escape, that you may be able to endure it" (1 Cor 10:13). The Lord wants to give us the power and the strength to resist wrongdoing and turn aside from it, but we can only appropriate that power by faith. I have often found that my failure to believe that I can resist sin is precisely what prevents me from actually resisting. If we give up and resign ourselves to our sin, we will not change. But if we believe in the Lord's power to help us conquer, we will change, perhaps not overnight, but eventually.

To renounce wrongdoing means to take action that will ensure righteousness in the future. You could hardly find a stronger admonition to renounce wrongdoing than Jesus' words in Mark's Gospel.

> And if your hand causes you to sin, cut it off; it is better for you to enter life maimed than with two hands to go to hell, to the unquenchable fire. And if your foot causes you to sin, cut it off; it is better for you to enter life lame than with two feet to be thrown into hell. And if your eye causes you to sin, pluck it out; it is better for you to enter the kingdom of God with one eye than with two eyes to be thrown into hell, where their worm does not die, and the fire is not quenched.
> (9:43-48)

Jesus tells us to renounce wrongdoing by dealing decisively with the means of temptation. Thus, a person with a spending problem should avoid roaming aimlessly around shopping malls; a person with a sexual-control problem should avoid magazine stands and provocative movies; and a person with a drinking or drug abuse problem should avoid the wrong type of parties and the wrong kind of friends. To avoid the occasions for sin is one significant step towards renouncing sin itself.

Another good way to resist temptation and overcome wrongdoing is to talk with a mature Christian man or woman about it and enlist their help. Wrongdoing thrives in the darkness but cowers in the light. The very act of talking about the problem can help us; it can put things in proper perspective, particularly if we've exaggerated the problem's seriousness and felt hopeless about our capacity to change. A mature Christian will probably be able to contribute wisdom from his or her experience that will provide encouragement and assistance.

It isn't enough to simply acknowledge our wrongdoing. If we are to truly repent and repair the damaged relationship, then we must also decide to turn from our wrongdoing and act differently in the future.

Step Three: Asking Forgiveness

The first two steps in this process of repentance deal solely with those of us who are the offenders: we have honestly admitted our wrongdoing and we have earnestly resolved to put it aside. But as yet we have not been reconciled to the offended party. The next two steps achieve and seal this reconciliation. Now we go to the offended party, and, having already acknowledged and renounced our wrong, proceed to repair the damaged relationship.

Perhaps you recognize as your own a train of thought that has often passed through my mind: "Look, Mark, you've already acknowledged and renounced this wrongdoing. That's enough, isn't it? (It was certainly hard enough.) There's no need to go to *him* and raise the whole issue again. It would be much better now to forget the whole affair and just press on." A very persuasive line of reasoning—especially since asking forgiveness from someone is such a humbling experience. The only problem with this line of thought is that it is false. Wrongdoing cannot be swept under the rug. Not only does it affect me and my spiritual condition, but it also damages my relationship with the Lord and with others. The relationship has been damaged, and now it must be repaired.

Jesus took reconciliation very seriously. If there is something wrong in a relationship, he commanded that we *go and get it right*. "So if you are offering your gift at the altar, and there remember that your brother has something against you, leave your gift there before the altar and *go*; first *be reconciled to your brother*, and then come and offer your gift" (Mt 5:23-24). "If your brother sins against you, *go* and tell him his fault, between you and him alone" (Mt 18:15). If someone else has a grievance against us, then we are to *go*; if we have a grievance against someone else, then we are to *go*;

above all else, *go*, seek out your brother, and be reconciled to him.

What do we say once we have gone to the person we've offended? Perhaps we can find a clue in a passage that we cited earlier.

> Take heed to yourselves; if your brother sins, rebuke him, and if he repents, forgive him; and if he sins against you seven times in the day, and turns to you seven times, and says, "I repent," you must forgive him. (Lk 17:3-4)

Notice two elements in this interchange: the expression of repentance and the granting of forgiveness. The expression of repentance is a statement of one's sorrow for the wrongdoing, but also a statement of one's desire and intention to change. Repentance should be expressed clearly, simply, and without embellishment: "Alice, I spoke harshly with you this morning for no good reason. It was wrong for me to do that. I do not want to do it again." This is what it means to say, "I repent."

The second element in the interchange is the granting of forgiveness. The type of forgiveness that brings full reconciliation cannot be granted until it is sought. Thus, if we want someone to forgive us, we should ask them to. Alice's friend should add to his expression of repentance a request for forgiveness: "Please forgive me for speaking harshly to you, Alice." Of course, now it's Alice's turn to respond to the Lord's teaching—he was as insistent that we forgive as he was that we seek forgiveness. "Forgive us our trespasses [debts], as we forgive those who trespass against us [our debtors]."

The closest thing to this kind of interchange in our society is the "I'm sorry"/"It's OK" approach to reconciliation. Now, this approach is certainly better than no approach at all. At least the command to *go* has been heeded. However, there are two problems with it. First of all, "I'm sorry" only communicates part of the meaning of "I repent." Though these words are used in several modern translations of Luke 17:4 (*The Jerusalem Bible*, *The New English Bible*, and *The New Testament in Modern English*), the phrase fails to communicate the aspect of renunciation discussed earlier. Second, the response "It's OK" implies that no wrong was done in the first place. People respond this way because they are embarrassed to be asked for forgiveness. But the truth is that something wrong was done. The person is asking that their action be forgiven, as a real debt is forgiven a debtor. Though the "I'm sorry"/"It's OK" approach may be acceptable in some situations, it is not the best way to achieve reconciliation.

The actual words we use in seeking reconciliation will be determined in part by the identity of the offended party. If the person is familiar with the process of repentance and forgiveness and is a Christian, one can clearly express repentance and ask forgiveness. (This obviously refers also to

God, who invented the whole thing.) If the person is less familiar with this process, it's probably better to stick with the "I'm sorry/It's OK" approach.

As I said earlier, seeking forgiveness is very difficult. When I began to ask others for forgiveness, the experience beforehand was excruciating but afterwards it was all joy. It is still difficult for me to own up to my wrong and ask another's forgiveness, but I must admit that it has grown much easier with practice. And the blessing following has not decreased a bit.

Step Four: Making Restitution

The fourth step in the process of repentance, and the second step of reconciliation, is to make restitution for the wrong that was done. Restitution means paying someone back for the damage your offense has inflicted on them. Though it isn't always possible to make restitution, we should do it whenever circumstances allow.

To make restitution is not to earn forgiveness. Instead, restitution expresses true repentance and the desire to repair the damage done in the relationship. One can see the principle of restitution at work in both the Old and New Testament. In Old Testament legislation dealing with property, we find the following commandment:

> If a man steals an ox or a sheep, and kills it or sells it, he shall pay five oxen for an ox, and four

sheep for a sheep. He shall make restitution; if he has nothing, then he shall be sold for his theft. If the stolen beast is found alive in his possession, whether it is an ox or an ass or a sheep, he shall pay double. (Ex 22:1; also see verses 5-6 and 14-15)

A similar law deals with issues that don't involve property.

When men quarrel and one strikes the other with a stone or with his fist and the man does not die but keeps his bed, then if the man rises again and walks abroad with his staff, he that struck him shall be clear; only he shall pay for the loss of his time, and shall have him thoroughly healed. (Ex 21:18)

In the New Testament we have the example of Zacchaeus, the chief tax collector of Jericho, who responded to the Lord with the following words:

"Behold, Lord, the half of my goods I give to the poor; and if I have defrauded any one of anything, I restore it fourfold." (Lk 19:8)

When Zacchaeus repented for the wrongdoing he had committed in the past, he offered restitution according to the Law to those who had been wronged.

The need for restitution is clearest in cases of theft or property damage. I know a man who stole several thousand dollars from his company before he became a Christian. Several years later, he returned, handed his former employers a check for the amount of money he had stolen, and asked their forgiveness. He was taken to a vice-president, who was amazed at his action and profoundly impressed with his Christian witness. Similarly, I know of others who have somehow damaged belongings borrowed from friends—a hunting rifle, a guitar, a tie, a punch bowl—and then repaired the damage by fixing the old article or buying a new one. In these types of situations, it isn't enough to say, "I repent"; one must also express one's repentance by acting to repair the damage that was done.

There are other cases of wrongdoing where it's appropriate to make restitution. Suppose that you have injured someone's reputation by saying something bad about them. In this case, you should explicitly correct your former remarks and counter them by saying something good about the person. Only then will your repentance be complete. If your wrongdoing has cost someone needed time, you can offer your own time as replacement. If you can't think of any other way to make restitution, you can always do a special favor for the offended party as an expression of your repentance.

The Lord wants us to repent eagerly and from the heart. If we earnestly desire right relationships, we will realize that restitution is not a burden but an opportunity to manifest our repentance and our eagerness to be reconciled to our brothers and sisters.

Conclusion

If this approach to reconciliation is to have its full effect, a body of people must adopt it and practice it together. For example, a family, church, or prayer group could decide to apply these principles. Everyone in the group would understand how to repent, ask forgiveness, grant forgiveness, and (when possible) make restitution. However, some modified form of this process of repentance and reconciliation can be fruitfully applied even to relationships that lack such a common understanding.

The Lord wants us to live as righteous men and women. This means that we must obey his commandments and love one another. But, since none of us are perfect and all of us stumble, living righteously means repairing wrongdoing when it occurs. Let us be quickly reconciled to God and one another. Such righteousness brings peace and freedom into our lives. We need not walk about carrying a burden of guilt that comes from having unresolved wrongdoing in our lives; we need not live in relationships that are strained by an accumulated burden of unresolved conflicts and grievances. Instead, we can live as righteous men and women who have been forgiven by the Lord and are reconciled to one another.

THREE

Living with a
Clear Conscience

FRED WALKED INTO Chuck and Sarah Miller's home and was welcomed warmly by the little company that gathered there weekly for prayer. Fred had become a Christian only two weeks before, mainly through the witness of Chuck, who was his professional colleague. He saw Chuck daily at work and was impressed with his courtesy, his generosity in offering help to his co-workers, his professional competence, and his concern for his family.

The prayer session began. After a brief moment of silence Chuck led out in prayer: "Lord, I know I am an abomination in your sight. I constantly fall into willful and malicious sin, profaning the blood of the covenant and meriting the full cup of your wrath. I stand in your presence as the foremost of sinners. My life is like a filthy rag, or like a can of garbage emitting a putrid stench. Have mercy on me, pitiful wretch that I am, and pardon my sin, for it is great."

Fred was astonished. In his eyes Chuck was a saint. He had never seen him unrighteously angry,

impatient, or intemperate in all the years he had
worked by his side. To what wrongdoing could his
prayer possibly refer?

Chuck was not in fact referring to specific
wrongdoing. He had been taught that Christians
should be humble and self-accusing, freely acknowledging their sin and their wickedness. Therefore
he worked hard to cultivate a sense of his own
moral corruption and unworthiness. And the
greatness of the challenge only heightened the
severity of his self-accusations.

Self-Condemnation: A Virtue?

Chuck's approach is quite common among
Christians. Many feel the need to proclaim that
they are sinful almost beyond hope, even though
their outward behavior and inner attitudes are
impeccably righteous. Self-reproach and self-
condemnation are elevated to the level of Christian
virtue. Is this in fact the way Christians should see
themselves?

To be conscious of one's sinful tendencies and
failings is indeed helpful. Such a consciousness
can make us more dependent upon God's grace
and mercy and more cautious about exposing
ourselves to situations that might cause us to sin.
Indeed there are blemishes in all our lives that
make us fall short of the perfection God originally
intended for his creatures.

Still, sinful tendencies are not the same as actual

wrongdoing. In this life we can never be totally free from the disordered inclinations and subtle imperfections that have their origin in human sin. But we can and should live free from actual wrongdoing. God's Spirit can fill our flawed earthen vessels, enabling us to live a righteous life. We should humbly acknowledge our flaws and our sinful tendencies, but our lives should still be fundamentally rooted in righteousness, bearing the fruit of a clear conscience rather than self-reproach.

Equating self-reproach and self-condemnation with Christian virtue has unfortunate consequences for those who suffer from an emotional problem with irrational feelings of guilt. They identify their emotional problem with an element of Christian sanctity. To do this is to become like deluded men who willingly bind themselves in chains of iron, thinking that their fetters are fine robes and precious jewels.

A close study of scripture reveals that self-condemnation is not, in fact, a Christian virtue. The biblical teaching on moral self-evaluation is quite different: we are summoned, in our new freedom in Christ, to live with a clear conscience.

A Clear Conscience

What does the word *conscience* mean? In modern usage the word is often used to refer to one's feelings of guilt or innocence. I have a bad conscience if I feel guilty and a good conscience if I feel innocent. But the word (in both Greek and English) derives from the word *consciousness* and refers to one's consciousness of guilt or innocence. Originally this consciousness was seen as more than just a feeling—it was also a rational judgment of the righteousness or unrighteousness of one's conduct. This is how scripture uses the term.

The scriptural teaching on conscience is simple and clear. After being reconciled to God in Christ we are supposed to live our lives with a good, or clear, conscience. This means that our conscience should declare us innocent rather than guilty. If, instead, it accuses us of evil (not just guilt feelings, but a rational judgment that we have done something wrong), then we should take pains to clear our conscience by repairing the wrong and living righteously in the future.

The best example of one who earnestly sought to live with a clear conscience is the Apostle Paul. It may surprise some to learn that Paul actually had what one scholar calls a "robust" conscience, and what Paul himself calls a "good" or "clear" conscience. Many people think of Paul as having a morbid and tormented sense of personal sin, but this is far from true. As the following passages indicate, Paul was confident that he was living in basic conformity to God's purpose for his life:

> And Paul, looking intently at the council, said, "Brethren, I have lived before God in all good conscience up to this day." (Acts 23:1)

For our boast is this, the testimony of our conscience that we have behaved in the world, and still more towards you, with holiness and godly sincerity, not by earthly wisdom but by the grace of God. (2 Cor 1:12)

You are witnesses, and God also, how holy and righteous and blameless was our behavior to you believers. (1 Thes 2:10)

In the first passage, Paul stands at his trial and defends himself against the accusations of the Jewish leaders. In the second and third passages, he may also be defending himself, but this time against members in the Corinthian and Thessalonian churches who dispute his apostolic authority. In each case his conclusion is the same: "I have behaved righteously towards God and towards man, and my conscience testifies to this fact" (see Heb 13:18 for a similar declaration).

At the same time, Paul also affirms that his conscience is not the ultimate authority. The ultimate authority is the Lord himself, and his judgment is the one that will stand.

This is how one should regard us, as servants of Christ and stewards of the mysteries of God. Moreover it is required of stewards that they be found trustworthy. But with me it is a very small thing that I should be judged by you or by any human court. I do not even judge myself. *I am not aware of anything against myself*, but I am not thereby acquitted. It is the Lord who judges. Therefore do not pronounce judgment before the time, before the Lord comes, who will bring to light the things now hidden in darkness and will disclose the purposes of the heart. Then every man will receive his commendation from God. (1 Cor 4:1-5)

The verb which is translated "I am not aware" is the word from which the Greek noun for conscience is derived. Paul thus asserts again that his conscience is clear. But he also asserts that only the Lord knows fully "the things now hidden in darkness" and the "purposes of the heart." With him stands the final judgment. We should seek to live now with a clear conscience, but we should also understand that the final verdict belongs to God.

But if Paul had such a clear conscience, what about his claim to be the "foremost of sinners" (1 Tm 1:15) and the "least of the apostles" (1 Cor 15:9)? Is he not in these passages reproaching himself for his sinful impulses? A closer look at both of these passages reveals that they refer to the same sin—Paul's persecution of the church before his conversion on the Damascus road.

I thank him who has given me strength for this, Christ Jesus our Lord, because he judged me faithful by appointing me to his service, though *I formerly blasphemed and persecuted and insulted him*; but I received mercy because I had acted ignorantly in unbelief, and the grace of our Lord overflowed for me with the faith and love that are in Christ Jesus. The saying is sure and worthy of full acceptance, that Christ Jesus came into the world to save sinners. *And I am the foremost of sinners*; but I received mercy for this reason, that in me, as the foremost, Jesus Christ might display his perfect patience for an example to those who were to believe in him for eternal life. (1 Tm 1:12-16)

When Jesus encountered Paul on the Damascus road, he asked him, "Saul, Saul, why do you persecute me?" (Acts 9:4). By persecuting the church, Saul was in fact persecuting Christ: "I formerly blasphemed and persecuted and insulted him." This is the gravest of sins, and it made Saul among the gravest of sinners. Yet the Lord had mercy on him and saved him as an example of his divine patience. Similarly, in 1 Corinthians 15:9-10 we read the following:

> For I am the least of the apostles, unfit to be called an apostle, *because I persecuted the church of God*. But by the grace of God I am what I am, and his grace towards me was not in vain.
>
> (1 Cor 15:9-10)

Paul does not belittle himself for his sins as a Christian. But he does remember his crime against the church, when he persecuted it as a non-Christian. He thanks God for his grace and mercy in calling him to be an apostle despite the enormity of his crime.

Paul's conscience as a Christian was clear, and

he took pains to keep it that way (Acts 24:16). He also exhorted others to do the same. "The aim of our charge is love that issues from a pure heart and a good conscience and sincere faith" (1 Tm 1:5). "Wage the good warfare, holding faith and a good conscience" (1 Tm 1:18-19; see 1 Pt 3:16 for a similar exhortation).

We should follow Paul's advice and example, and strive to live in such a way that our conscience is clear.

A Counterfeit Virtue

It is thus apparent that the Bible does not urge us on to the path of self-condemnation. If we have sinned, we should repent and be reconciled to God and our brother or sister. If we have not sinned, we should rejoice that God's grace has preserved us in righteousness. We should never pretend that our righteousness is actually unrighteousness. To bewail sin we have not committed is to live in a spiritual fantasy world and to insult the grace of God.

FOUR

Contrition or Condemnation?

ONE REASON WHY many Christians consider self-condemnation a virtue is that they mistake it for something else. They mistake self-condemnation for contrition—sorrow. Now, Christians have always valued sorrow for sin. It is an important element in the act of repentance. But if we lose sight of the distinction between self-condemnation and contrition, we run the risk of nursing a destructive emotional problem as though it were a precious spiritual blessing.

Godly Grief and Worldly Grief

In his second letter to the Corinthians, Paul discusses two types of grief—godly grief and worldly grief. His remarks can help us understand the distinction between contrition and self-condemnation:

> For even if I made you sorry with my letter, I do not regret it (though I did regret it), for I see that that letter grieved you, though only for a while. As it is, I rejoice, not because you were grieved, but because *you were grieved into*

repenting; for you felt a godly grief, so that you suffered no loss through us. *For godly grief produces a repentance that leads to salvation and brings no regret, but worldly grief produces death.* For see what earnestness this godly grief has produced in you, what eagerness to clear yourselves, what indignation, what alarm, what longing, what zeal, what punishment! At every point you have proved yourselves guiltless in the matter. (2 Cor 7:8-11)

Paul's correspondence with the Corinthian church reveals the stormy ups-and-downs of their relationship. At a certain point Paul wrote them a letter rebuking their wrongdoing and calling them to repentance. Later, one of Paul's assistants, Titus, brought Paul the news that his letter had produced its intended effect. In the passage quoted above the apostle praises the Corinthians for their response and points out the benefits of "godly grief."

What is this grief that Paul praises? The most important feature of this grief is that it "produces a repentance that leads to salvation." It leads to a change in behavior, a change for the better. The ultimate result of godly grief is salvation—the salvation which comes on the last day to the servants of God who have repented of their sin and embraced in faith their new life in Christ. On the other hand, worldly grief produces a very different kind of fruit—death. Worldly grief leads to no positive change in behavior, no turning from sin and self-centeredness to the Lord of Righteousness. Instead, it sends one plummeting down a deadly precipice.

In scripture, godly grief—sorrow for sin—is an important aspect of repentance. The customs followed when repenting of serious wrongdoing were the same customs followed when mourning for the dead. Expressing mourning and grief for the wrong committed was another way of *renouncing* the wrong. The following passage from the book of Jonah serves as a good example of this:

Then the word of the Lord came to Jonah the second time, saying, "Arise, go to Nineveh, that great city, and proclaim to it the message that I tell you." So Jonah arose and went to Nineveh, according to the word of the Lord. Now Nineveh was an exceedingly great city, three days' journey in breadth. Jonah began to go into the city, going a day's journey. And he cried, "Yet forty days, and Nineveh shall be overthrown!" And the people of Nineveh believed God; *they proclaimed a fast, and put on sackcloth,* from the greatest of them to the least of them.

Then tidings reached the king of Nineveh, and he arose from his throne, *removed his robe, and covered himself with sackcloth, and sat in ashes.* And he made proclamation and published through Nineveh, "By the decree of the king and his nobles: Let neither man nor beast, herd nor flock, taste anything; *let them not feed, or drink water, but let man and beast be covered with sackcloth, and let them cry mightily to God; yea, let every one turn from his evil way and from the violence which is in his hands.* Who knows, God may yet repent and turn from his fierce anger, so that we perish not?"

When God saw what they did, how they turned from their evil way, God repented of the evil which he had said he would do to them; and he did not do it. (Jon 3:1-10)

The people of Nineveh responded to Jonah's prophetic warning by repenting and praying for mercy. Their repentance expressed two important things: (1) mourning and grief over their sin, and (2) a turning from their "evil way," an actual change in the way they behaved. This is an example of a godly grief that "produces a repentance that leads to salvation and brings no regret."

Godly grief derives from a concern for the offended parties (the Lord and, perhaps, another person) and also from a concern for our relationship with them. It is directed towards the wrong-doing, rather than towards ourselves; we mourn for what we have done and for the damage that has resulted, rather than mourning for how stupid and wicked we are. Most importantly, godly grief issues in change. It helps us become reconciled to the offended party and to resolve firmly never to repeat our wrong.

Self-condemnation, on the other hand, derives from self-concern. It is directed towards ourselves, not towards the wrong. It leads to self-hatred, self-rejection, discouragement, depression, and self-pity. Instead of resulting in a positive behavioral change, self-condemnation actually stands in the way of such a change. Self-condemnation produces "death" rather than "repentance" and "salvation."

It's easy for me to tell when I am responding to my sin with self-condemnation rather than with true contrition. When I am yielding to self-condemnation, I lose the motivation to do anything. I do not want to serve other people—in fact, I do not want even to relate to other people. Of course, the last thing I want to do is to pray or read scripture or act "spiritual." My main desire is to be alone and sulk. On the other hand, true contrition leads me first to prayer and earnest confession of my wrongdoing. It makes me desire more of God's grace in my life so that I can live more righteously before him. After true contrition, my service to other people increases. Contrition leads to repentance and life, but self-condemnation leads only to introspection and death.

In Matthew 26:69—27:5 we see a stark contrast between godly grief and worldly grief. First, we see Peter deny Jesus. Then he hears the cock crow and remembers the prophecy Jesus spoke earlier that evening: "Before the cock crows, you will deny me three times." Recognizing the full import of what he has just done, Peter goes out and weeps bitterly. This grief brings a repentance that helps Peter become the new man we see in the book of

Acts—bold, mature, and ready to suffer for his Lord.

Next, we see Judas Iscariot, the betrayer of the Lord. His role had also been known and prophesied by his Master. Like Peter, Judas also grieves over his great wrongdoing. He knows that he is guilty: "I have sinned in betraying innocent blood." But where does his remorse lead? "And he went and hanged himself." Judas' grief only leads him to death.

Self-condemnation leads not to repentance but to introspection and discouragement. It actually impedes repentance. Therefore, our response to self-condemnation should be clear and decisive— we should repent of it, turn aside from it, resist it. It is not a spiritual fruit to be cultivated, but a weed to be rooted out of our lives.

The Heavenly Courtroom

Contrition and condemnation are not merely human psychological realities. They also have a spiritual basis. The Holy Spirit brings conviction of sin and genuine contrition, and Satan—the Evil Spirit—brings condemnation.

The spiritual realities underlying contrition and condemnation can be illustrated by a courtroom analogy, an analogy common in scripture. God Almighty is the judge, and we are the defendants. As we stand in fear and perhaps embarrassment before his all-knowing eye, another character appears on the scene—Satan, the prosecuting attorney. He carries in his hand a large scroll with our name printed on it in red, and he begins to unravel the scroll and read it to the judge and to us. Written on the scroll are all of the wrongs, major and minor, that we have ever committed, phrased in the most bitter and incriminating language. Satan reads the words of the scroll spitefully and with contempt, and concludes by pleading with the judge to show no mercy to the villain who stands in his awesome presence.

This type of picture of the heavenly courtroom is found in several passages of scripture. In the first chapter of Job, Satan comes into the presence of God. After hearing God boast of Job's righteousness, Satan begins to accuse Job. In Zechariah 3:1 something similar happens: "Then he showed me Joshua the high priest standing before the angel of the Lord, and Satan standing at his right hand to accuse him." In Revelation 12:10 Satan is called "the accuser of our brethren, who accuses them day and night before our God." Even his name— Satan—has a meaning that confirms his identity as the prosecutor: It denotes an accuser in a court of law.

The prosecuting attorney has rested his case, and the verdict seems certain. We now have the opportunity to defend ourselves, but what shall we say? Then the final character appears on the scene. Robed in heavenly splendor, he stands by our side and pleads our cause. He represents us before God and rebukes the insolence of the prosecuting attorney. His gracious intercession wins our justification, and we are acquitted.

> My little children, I am writing this to you so that you may not sin; but if any one does sin, we have an *advocate* with the Father, Jesus Christ the righteous; and he is the expiation for our sins, and not for ours only but also for the sins of the whole world. (1 Jn 2:1-2)

The advocate [in Greek, paraclete] is Jesus Christ, the attorney for the defense. He intercedes for us and pleads our cause.

We also have another advocate, the Holy Spirit:

> I will pray the Father, and he will give you another Counselor [in Greek, paraclete] to be with you for ever, even the Spirit of truth, whom the world cannot receive, because it neither sees him nor knows him; you know him, for he dwells with you, and will be in you.
> (Jn 14:16-17)

The Holy Spirit also stands by our side and comes to our aid. The accusations of Satan cannot possibly carry the day, for our advocates are far greater than he.

The prosecuting attorney points out sins and portrays them in their worst possible light, all so that we might be condemned and destroyed. The advocate also points out our sins, but his intention is to bring us to repentance and salvation. The effects of contrition and self-condemnation correspond to the intentions of these two attorneys—one aims to save us, the other to destroy us.

Of course, this courtroom analogy has its limitations. God the Father does not really stand by impassively while Satan accuses us, nor does Jesus have to argue persuasively in order to convince the Father to show us mercy. However, the analogy does illustrate an important truth: Satan is out to destroy us, and accusation is one of his favorite tactics. The Holy Spirit will bring us to contrition, but never to self-condemnation. When we yield to self-condemnation, we subject ourselves to the destructive power of the father of lies.

It's important for Christians to distinguish between contrition and self-condemnation. Failure to make this distinction often causes us to honor as a virtue what is in fact the devil's tool. With the light of God's wisdom we can uncover Satan's clever subterfuge and turn to the road that leads away from death and towards repentance and salvation.

FIVE

Righteous or Overscrupulous?

A YOUNG MAN ONCE came to me desiring to unburden his conscience. He had a strong sense of guilt and felt that much in his life was wrong. He proceeded to list off a series of trivial faults, mistakes, and minor sins that did not impress me in the least. At a certain point I could not help but interrupt: "Look, Phil, if you want to impress me with your sinfulness you really should do something more seriously wrong, or at least something juicier and more sensational." At first his face registered confusion and disbelief at my comment, but he quickly broke out into a laugh. We then discussed his situation and came to a more sober and accurate estimation of where his life really stood. He left the conversation greatly relieved and with a clearer vision of the things in his life that really did need to change.

Many Christians fail to live with a clear conscience because they become overly scrupulous in their zeal for righteousness. Certainly one can never be overly zealous for righteousness. However, one can become so scrupulously concerned about being righteous that one sees wrongdoing everywhere, even where it is not. Being over-scrupulous entails a loss of perspective and a false sense of proportion; we are unable to determine which of our failings should be taken less seriously and which more. Consequently, many Christians (like Phil) grieve earnestly over faults that they should pass over more casually with a good-hearted resolution to improve.

Christians who have problems with self-con-demnation are usually overscrupulous as well. God's expectations seem unreachable to them, and therefore they live in a constant state of disappointment with themselves for not measuring up. In fact, God does have high expectations for us. But they are reasonable, given that his power is at work within us. He does not expect us to be flawless, but he does expect us to be righteous. If we are to put aside self-condemnation and live with a clear conscience, then we must grasp with greater clarity what it really means to live in righteousness; it may not mean what we had scrupulously thought it meant.

Identifying Wrongdoing

What is wrongdoing? How is it to be defined? How are we to know when we have committed it?

The word *wrongdoing* refers to acts that we commit in either thought, word, or deed which violate God's standard of righteousness and for which he holds us accountable. It does not refer to the inclination towards evil found in all people (as some would hold the word *sin* does), but only to the occasions when we accept and act upon this inclination. As discussed earlier, all wrongdoing damages our relationship with God and sometimes our relationships with other people. If we are to live righteously before the Lord, we must repent of all wrongdoing and we must responsibly repair the relationships that our wrongdoing has damaged.

Perhaps the best way to illustrate the nature of wrongdoing is to describe those things that are often mistakenly identified with it. The following do *not* constitute wrongdoing: (1) temptations of feeling or thought; (2) small faults; (3) idiosyncrasies; (4) mistakes; (5) failures in performance; and (6) weaknesses. We will now look at each in turn.

Temptations of feeling or thought. We are not responsible for every emotion that we might feel or every thought that might enter our heads. Wrong thoughts and feelings are temptations provided by Satan or by our flesh. As in all tests, the crucial factor is how we respond to these thoughts and feelings. Do we allow that stray thought that walked into our mind like an entertainer on stage to develop into a *train* of thought that we gaze on and enjoy? If so, we are guilty of wrongdoing. Do we indulge in feelings that inhibit us from obeying God's commandments and loving our brothers and sisters? If so, we are guilty of wrongdoing. The appearance of such thoughts and feelings is beyond our control, and can even be handled with a sense of humor. But the cultivation of these thoughts and feelings is something for which we are accountable.

It's especially important to recall this principle when dealing with thoughts and feelings connected to sexual desire or hostility. We all experience sexual thoughts and sexual desires, sometimes even of a grotesque and perverse nature; we all experience occasional thoughts that are critical of others, and we may even desire to hurt someone. The appearance of a sexual fantasy or a malicious thought, uninvited and unwelcome, is not an act of wrongdoing. If the fantasy is indulged rather than resisted, however, we become responsible for our act. The initial thoughts and feelings, though not a part of God's perfect plan, are not wrongdoing in themselves. They are but temptations that test and prove us. The main issue is how we respond to them.

This truth is aptly illustrated in a saying from the Desert Fathers, a group of men who participated in an ascetical renewal movement in the early centuries of the Christian church:

An old man said to a brother, "The devil is the enemy and you yourself are the house. The enemy never stops throwing all that he finds into your house, pouring all sorts of impurities over it. It is your part not to neglect throwing them outside again. If you do not do this the house will be filled with all sorts of impurities and you will no longer be able to get inside. But all that the other begins to throw in, you should throw out again little by little, and by the grace of Christ your house will remain pure."[6]

We cannot keep Satan from throwing impurities into our house, but we can fling them out again as soon as we find them.

Small faults. We all have small character flaws and imperfections that are most visible to those we live with. Some of us talk a bit too much and listen a bit too little. Some of us tend to be untidy and disordered in our appearance and our personal habits. Some of us are too loud and rambunctious, and some of us are too retiring and anti-social. These behavior patterns are all faults, and we should do what we can to change them, but they are usually not wrongdoing.

We all have some small faults, and some of these will be with us until the day we die. Of course we can improve over the years, eliminating some flaws and minimizing others; but we will never be flawless. Some small imperfection will always remain to try our husband or wife for years on end and produce in them the blessed fruit of patience and forebearance! But wrongdoing, on the other hand, is something that we can be free of. In fact, God expects us to live a life free of wrongdoing. While some small habits and behavior patterns will take years of hard work to change, and some may never change, wrongdoing is something God expects us to put aside and never pick up again.

Idiosyncrasies. Idiosyncrasies are those little quirks in our personality and behavior that are so harmless that they don't even qualify as weaknesses or faults. Some people may find our particular idiosyncrasies charming and delightful, while others may find them excruciatingly annoying. It's all a matter of taste. Obviously, even though they may annoy some people, such idiosyncrasies are not wrongdoing.

Sometimes we should work to overcome our idiosyncrasies for the sake of those closest to us or for the sake of some service that the Lord gives us. For example, several years ago I lived with several single Christian men. One day a couple of men complained to me about the way I climbed the stairs. They said that they could hear me stomping up the stairs regardless of where they were in the house, and it greatly annoyed them. One of them even offered the comment that my heavy tread might damage the structure of the house! Now, it would have been futile for me to search through the scriptures for some commandment regulating one's conduct on stairs. Nonetheless, I was eager to change the habit if it so perturbed my brothers in Christ. My elephant stomping did not become the light tread of a deer overnight, but within a month I had changed enough to satisfy my friends.

Sometimes our idiosyncrasies, like our faults, should change. But idiosyncrasies are not wrongdoing and should not be related to as wrongdoing.

Mistakes. Like faults and idiosyncrasies, mistakes are unavoidable. They are an inevitable part of our frail human condition. Like faults, we should avoid them whenever possible; we should learn from our mistakes, trying not to repeat them. Sometimes mistakes cause damage to someone; we should then express sorrow to that person for our mistake. However, generally speaking, mistakes should not be classified as wrongdoing.

Recently, I was being driven by a friend to a meeting that was two hundred miles from our home. I was leafing through some papers in preparation for the meeting as we entered the Ohio Turnpike. Looking up, I was aghast to see that my friend had mistakenly turned on to the ramp heading west. Our destination lay east! I quickly studied the turnpike map and learned to my chagrin that our next exit was twenty-five miles ahead; we would need to drive fifty miles out of our way, and we would arrive close to an hour late for our meeting. My friend was deeply sorry for his mistake, which was largely attributable to his unfamiliarity with midwestern America. His mistake was regrettable, but it was not wrongdoing.

Some mistakes, however, may be classified as

wrongdoing. For example, mistakes that are made because of serious negligence or irresponsibility may be wrongdoing. In such cases the mistake itself is not so much the problem as the negligence or irresponsibility that caused it.

Failures in performance. None of us perform our daily tasks perfectly. There is always room for growth and improvement. But failing in our performance is not the same as committing wrongdoing.

I learned this lesson during my years as a student. Since I was highly achievement-oriented, I would aim for excellence in all my studies, and feel discouraged and self-condemned whenever I failed to attain my goal. For me, to get a "C" on an exam or research paper was like being convicted of armed robbery or manslaughter—a serious offense! As I began to grow in my understanding of scripture and the ways of God, I realized that my perspective was greatly distorted. If I did my best but was unable to achieve a glorious success, God was not angry with me, and I should not be angry with myself. I began to learn that a failure in performance is not the same as an act of wrongdoing.

Many times we can learn from our failures in performance so that we do not fail again. In some cases, our failures may indicate that we lack the gifts needed to perform the task—this is another type of learning experience. Regardless, we must all cope with failures in performance—they cannot be avoided. Though such failures may be painful, we should understand clearly that they are not wrongdoing.

Weaknesses. All of us are subject to the limitations and weaknesses of our pre-resurrection human nature. The Lord imparts strength to our body, mind, and spirit (Phil 4:13), but we never reach a point where we are totally liberated from human weakness. Weakness is not a Christian ideal, but neither is it wrongdoing.

Many people feel guilty when their bodies are weakened by an accident or illness. Though physical infirmity sometimes follows from wrongdoing, not all sickness comes as a consequence of our personal sin, and sickness itself is not something to feel guilty about. We should strive to be healthy, but we should not identify illness with wrongdoing.

Similarly, we should not feel guilty about emotional weakness. Many of us suffer from excessive fear, insecurity, lack of confidence, or some other emotional disorder. Though these problems can lead us into wrongdoing if we are not careful, they are not in themselves culpable acts. We may experience many feelings of fear or insecurity without doing anything wrong. We should strive to overcome these weaknesses, but we should not feel guilty about them.

Neither should we feel guilty about weaknesses

in gift or ability. I am clumsy with my hands and have always been dreadful at art, handicrafts, carpentry, and mechanical repairs. I would like to do better in these areas, but I don't feel guilty about my limitations. Others lack skill when it comes to writing, speaking, organizing, and planning. We should strive to strengthen those of our skills that are weak, but we should not feel guilty about them.

Many of us suffer from self-condemnation because we mistakenly think of temptations, small faults, idiosyncrasies, mistakes, failures in performance, and weaknesses as wrongdoing. We are overscrupulous, and we identify every imperfection as unrighteousness. If we can grow in our understanding of what wrongdoing is and is not, we will be able to overcome self-condemnation without losing any of our commendable zeal for righteousness.

Biblical Perfection

The New Testament uses a word that causes many of us to tremble: it is the word *perfect*. "You, therefore, must be perfect, even as your heavenly father is perfect" (Mt 5:48). How are we, flawed and frail human beings, to reach such perfection? This command to be perfect especially shakes the overscrupulous among us and stirs them to redouble their efforts to remove every blemish.

If we are to understand this biblical injunction properly, we must explore the meaning of the word *perfect*. In normal English usage this word means *flawless, without fault or defect*. We speak of an unblemished diamond as perfect, or of a precisely painted portrait as a perfect likeness. Thus we interpret this biblical command as meaning that we are to be absolutely flawless— which is, of course, impossible. Most of us become reconciled to this impossibility, but some of the overscrupulous among us keep on trying.

The Greek word for *perfect* in the New Testament means something very different. It is often translated *mature* or *complete*. The perfect man is the one who is fully developed, lacking nothing essential.

> You know that the testing of your faith produces steadfastness. And let steadfastness have its full effect, that you may be *perfect* and complete, lacking in nothing. (Jas 1:3-4)

The New Testament does not teach that we are to be flawless, but that we are to live as mature sons and daughters of God, obeying his commandments and advancing his kingdom. Our "perfection" as children of God means that we should be free from wrongdoing. When we commit wrongdoing, we repair it. Christian perfection in scripture does not mean freedom from internal temptations, small faults, or mistakes. It does mean that we live righteously before the Father, trying to please him in everything. We need not be overscrupulous in order to fulfill the command to be perfect.

SIX

Taking Charge

SCRIPTURE TEACHES THAT we should live with a clear conscience. The Lord doesn't intend us to live in bondage to feelings of self-condemnation and self-reproach. Nevertheless, many of us do fall prey to these ruthless taskmasters. What can we do to obtain our freedom?

The first thing we need to do is to take charge. For years many of us have been docile, obedient slaves to self-condemnation, cowering submissively before its commands. We must begin our liberation campaign by recognizing clearly that this master has no rightful authority over us. We must then proceed to aggressively oppose its rule. The Lord will give us the wisdom and the power of the Holy Spirit to win for us victory and freedom.[7]

Applying the Basic Teaching

Let's review what we've learned so far. Much of what we've said is foundational for overcoming self-condemnation.

First, there is no substitute for living righteously. The fundamental problem underlying the sad condition of the human race is not the bondage caused by our tyrannical superegos, but the bondage caused by sin. We are sinful men and women, who need to be reconciled to our heavenly Father. Once we are reconciled to him in Christ, we can experience the life of the kingdom of God—"For the kingdom of God is not food and drink but righteousness and peace and joy in the Holy Spirit; he who thus serves Christ is acceptable to God and approved by men" (Rom 14:17-18). We cannot live in sin and expect the Lord to help us overcome our problem with self-condemnation. Only a righteous life lived in the power of the Holy Spirit will enable us to break the chains of self-condemnation.

Second, an essential part of living in righteousness is repairing the wrong we do. If we fail to repair our wrongdoing, it will gain power over us, dissolving our relationships and handing us over to the just accusations of our conscience. But if we do repair our wrongdoing, we will enjoy the fruit of right relationships; we will also stand on a solid foundation to resist the condemnation of the enemy.

In particular, we should be careful to ask forgiveness from those whom we have offended. It has been my experience that people suffering from self-condemnation tend to be especially reluctant to ask forgiveness. Yet to receive forgiveness can be the most healing and liberating element of the entire reconciliation process. Though it involves humbling ourselves, we neglect it at our own peril.

Sometimes our problem with self-condemnation

is connected to wrongdoing that we have committed in the past. In many cases this wrongdoing cannot be repaired—the offended party has moved away or is no longer living. However, if we have the opportunity to repair serious wrongdoing committed in the past, we should seize it. Once again, this is a difficult task that holds out a great reward.

Third, if we want to live with a clear conscience, we should avoid being overscrupulous. Another name for this malady is "the eggshell syndrome." This term came to me one day as I was thinking about a friend of mine who is often burdened by self-condemnation. He is so scrupulous about his conduct that he sometimes seems like a man walking on a field of eggshells, determined not to crush a single one. This preoccupation with avoiding mistakes can lead him to be tense, inhibited, and frequently self-condemned. The next time I saw him I decided to give him some advice: "Stomp on those eggshells, Chris, stomp on them!" He did not immediately comprehend the meaning of my counsel, so I explained the eggshell syndrome. In this young man's case, putting aside overscrupulosity has been crucial to overcoming self-condemnation. This is also the case for many of us.

Fourth and most importantly, we must expose self-condemnation for what it is, refusing to let it masquerade as a Christian virtue or as objective self-evaluation. We need to realize that self-condemnation is a trick commonly used by Satan;

then we need to see how it works practically in our own lives. Like other self-image problems, self-condemnation draws much of its power from the illusion that it speaks the truth rather than lies—"I don't have a problem with self-condemnation; I simply deserve to be condemned." If we have repented, this is a lie. If we have not repented, then we should repent and make it a lie.

This fourth point is essential if we are to triumph over self-condemnation. Otherwise we are like slaves who are deceived into believing that their cruel master is an honest friend. We cannot conquer self-condemnation unless we expose its true identity and raise our arms to fight. But how do we fight? What are the main weapons in our spiritual arsenal?

Faith, Repentance, and Authority

Three main spiritual weapons, if wielded deftly, will enable us to overcome self-condemnation. They are faith, repentance, and authority. In fact, these are the basic weapons to be used in *every* area of the Christian life. We must always begin by believing God's promises and appropriating his power, by turning from wrong patterns of thought, word, and deed, and by taking authority over the work of Satan.

Faith. As Paul writes in Ephesians, take "the shield of faith, with which you can quench all the flaming darts of the evil one" (6:16). What do we put our faith in? Our faith rests first and foremost on God himself, whose commitment to us is so great that he *wants* to help us, and whose power is so great that he *is able* to help us. We also put our faith in God's word, which is given to us in scripture. It is utterly trustworthy and reliable.

God himself has taken the initiative to establish a relationship with us, and he continues to take the initiative to guide and shape our lives according to his purpose. The way we respond to God's sovereign initiative is through exercising faith. We believe that he wants to sanctify, strengthen, lead, and equip us as his servants, and we thereby lay aside discouragement and fearfulness, yielding ourselves trustingly into his hands. We have put our confidence in a God who is able and willing, and we should not limit what he might want to do in our lives.

If we have put our faith in God, then we will ask him to help us overcome our difficulty with self-condemnation. We will meditate on the merciful attributes of his character, recognizing that he is a God who forgives and helps. We will not look to ourselves for strength to resist the enemy but will look instead to the power supplied by the Holy Spirit. We will also not trust ourselves for our righteousness but will look to him who fills us "with the fruits of righteousness which come through Jesus Christ, to the glory and praise of God" (Phil 1:11).

We will also put our faith in God's word. This is particularly important, for the scripture speaks forcefully about forgiveness and condemnation. Consider this passage from the first letter of John: "If we say we have no sin, we deceive ourselves, and the truth is not in us. If we confess our sins, he is faithful and just, and will forgive our sins and cleanse us from all unrighteousness" (1 Jn 1:8-9). Thus, if we do something wrong, we should not respond by wallowing in a pit of self-condemnation. Instead, we should run to God our Father, confessing our sin and expressing our repentance. If we do this, God's word tells us, we can expect him to forgive us graciously.

Why do we not want to enter God's presence in prayer after we sin? We know God is angry with us, and we don't expect him to forgive our sin. How many times have we stood or knelt in God's presence, confessing our sin, yet feeling a horrible conviction that we weren't forgiven? We reason that, since God will not forgive us, we certainly cannot forgive ourselves. But in reality, it's because we cannot forgive ourselves that we refuse God's forgiveness. So we try to punish ourselves emotionally with self-condemnation until we think we have earned God's forgiveness.

If we put our faith in God's word and not in our feelings, then we will know with certainty that we are forgiven as soon as we turn to God in repentance. We should grieve for our wrongdoing, not because we believe that God will hold it against us for eternity, but because we do not want to offend him in any way. We grieve because our action has displeased the Lord, but we rejoice because we know that our Father forgives us when we call upon him.

Faith in God and in his word gives us a sure conviction of where we stand. We are not pleading our case before a cruel and heartless judge, but before our Creator and Redeemer; the Son of God stands at our side to intercede for us.

> What then shall we say to this? If God is for us, who is against us? He who did not spare his own Son but gave him up for us all, will he not also give us all things with him? Who shall bring any charge against God's elect? It is God who justifies; who is to condemn? Is it Christ Jesus, who died, yes, who was raised from the dead, who is at the right hand of God, who indeed intercedes for us? Who shall separate us from the love of Christ? (Rom 8:31-35)

God delights in a contrite and repentant heart. To yield to self-condemnation is to call into question his character and his word. Let us, instead, put our faith in him by claiming the forgiveness he has promised us.

Repentance. We need to embrace the truth of our forgiveness and our right standing before God. However, we also need to turn aside from the self-condemning lies that so easily deceive us. We actually need to repent of self-condemnation.

Self-condemnation is an act of unbelief. It leads to patterns of behavior that diminish our love for the Lord, our love for other people, and the effectiveness of our Christian service. We become tangled in a web of introspection and self-pity, bound by the sticky threads of self-concern. There is nothing praiseworthy about self-condemnation, but there is much in it that is evil. Therefore, once we recognize self-condemnation for what it is, we should decide to turn from it as we would turn from sin itself.

The great power of self-condemnation comes from our own willingness to cooperate with it. I once knew a woman who had committed some serious wrongdoing earlier in her life. Later, she became a Christian and renounced her former manner of living. Nonetheless, she remained bound by the sense of guilt occasioned by her former sins. No matter how insistently I assured her of God's forgiveness, she continued to feel self-condemned. Part of her problem stemmed from a lack of faith, but another part came from a lack of repentance—not repentance for her sins, but for yielding to condemning lies. We must turn *to* God in faith, but we must also turn *away from* the deception of self-condemnation. Self-condemnation cannot hold us if we refuse to believe what it tells us.

Authority. As we saw earlier, accusation is the work of Satan. He delights to accuse us before our Father, and he also delights to accuse us before ourselves. If he can make us despair, he might even lead us into serious sin and a life separated from God. Failing this, he can at least make life miserable for us and for those around us. We should recognize here the work of our spiritual foe; we should not be "ignorant of his designs" (2 Cor 2:11).

The crucial truth here is that we need not be subject to the lies of Satan. God has not given Satan authority over us, but, astounding as it seems, has instead given us authority over him. "Behold, I have given you authority to tread upon serpents and scorpions, and over all the power of the enemy; and nothing shall hurt you" (Lk 10:19). What does it mean to have such authority? It means that we can take action against Satan, and that God's power will back us up, much like a judge can take action, knowing that the police will back him up. We confront Satan and his lies from a position of strength, not a position of weakness.

Sometimes we may find it especially difficult to turn aside from self-condemnation. We want to repent of listening to Satan's accusations, but they seem to have a special power over us. In such cases it helps to clearly and verbally address Satan in the name and authority of Jesus Christ, letting him know that the power of God is on *our* side. Doing this will often enable us to break the hold of self-condemnation and to appropriate in faith the truth of God's promises.

For too long, many of us have lain prostrate on the ground with the foot of self-condemnation on our neck. Now the Lord wants us to begin to take charge. We can do this by seizing the weapons he has given us—the weapons of faith, repentance, and authority. We should wield them skillfully against our enemy. After a time he will inevitably retreat.

Abandoning Resentment

Before concluding this chapter, we should look at one last way to overcome self-condemnation. This method is less direct than the others we have considered, but it is no less important. It involves abandoning resentment.

For many people, self-condemnation is tied to resentment. Our self-reproach is only one side of a coin; on the other side is our reproach of others. We complain bitterly about the poor treatment we have received from our family, our employer, our church, our school, our friends. At the same time, we know the offenses we have committed, and we burn with self-reproach. The harsh judgment we mete out to others is the same stiff penalty we exact from ourselves.

We must abandon our resentment. Resentment is like a poison that gradually eats away at our spiritual life. It has many evil effects, one of which is bondage to self-condemnation. We must repent of our grudges, our bitterness, our critical and judgmental spirit, and take on the mind of Jesus Christ, who pleaded with his Father for the forgiveness of his enemies' sin. Only then will we receive the grace to overcome our bondage to self-condemnation. Only then will we know with assurance the Father's forgiveness.

SEVEN

Freeing One Another

WE EMBARK ON the road to overcoming self-condemnation by taking charge of our life and starting to fight. However, we will probably not win full freedom unless we receive some help from others. This principle applies to most areas of our Christian life—we can only move so far on our own; we need the help of our brothers and sisters to move farther. In some cases our first step in taking charge should be to seek the help of another.

When God first created us, he intended us to be creatures who relied on each other for the satisfaction of our basic needs. Our new life in Christ, the new creation, also joins us to others in interdependent relationships of love and service. Without each other, we cannot become what the Lord wants us to be. This truth applies immediately to our attempt to overcome self-condemnation. God wants to free us from self-condemnation through the help of others, and he wants to free others through us.

Seeking Help

Our brothers and sisters in Christ can perform two important services that will help us fight self-condemnation. The first is to hear us as we confess our wrongdoing; the second is to help us determine where wrongdoing has occurred. But in order to receive their help, we must first ask for it. This sounds simple enough, but it's something that many of us fail to do. We will not receive unless we ask; we will not find unless we seek; the door will not open unless we knock.

Confessing wrongdoing.   We have already talked about confessing wrongdoing when we have offended one another, and we have talked about confessing wrongdoing to God. Here I want to make a new recommendation: if we have a problem with self-condemnation, it can be very helpful to confess to a brother or sister in Christ, even if they were not the person wronged. Scripture supports this approach. Consider this passage from James, which is primarily concerned with prayer for healing.

Is any among you sick? Let him call for the elders of the church, and let them pray over him, anointing him with oil in the name of the Lord; and the prayer of faith will save the sick man, and the Lord will raise him up; and if he has committed sins, he will be forgiven. There-

fore confess your sins to one another, and pray
for one another, that you may be healed.

(Jas 5:14-16)

Scripture often connects sickness to sin, and
healing to forgiveness. Not all sickness arises as a
consequence of sin ("and *if* he has committed
sins"), but it can sometimes be caused by sin.
Christians who are sick are thus instructed both to
call for the elders to pray over them and to *confess*
their sins to them, since these might be the source
of the physical affliction. God will respond by
healing the sickness and forgiving the sin.

Confessing our wrongdoing to our brothers and
sisters has special power to help us appropriate
God's forgiveness and to heal the various consequences of our wrongdoing. I have certainly
found this principle to hold true in my own
experience. Several years ago I heard a teaching on
"living in the light," a term adapted from 1 John
1:5-10. The teacher used the expression to
encourage Christians to share their wrongdoing
freely with one another. I probably broke into a
sweat just listening to this teaching, for I did not
relish the thought of parading my closeted
skeletons before my brothers. In the following
week, I spent a couple of nervous days examining
one or two of my ugliest skeletons, debating with
myself whether to bring them out before a brother.
I finally decided to give it a try. I made an
appointment with a Christian man whose wisdom

and maturity I especially admired, and prepared to share with him the horrible things no one else had ever heard about me.

From one point of view the appointment was a total letdown. My friend was not scandalized by anything that I shared; in fact, he even chuckled once or twice. My defenses, my fears, my shame—all were totally disarmed and set aside. I entered the meeting with the belief that my friend would never fully respect me again, and departed knowing as never before the forgiveness of God in Jesus Christ and the true mettle of my brother's love. A letdown of sorts, but certainly one of the most pleasant letdowns of my life.

I learned several things from this incident about the benefits that come from confessing our wrongdoing to one another. First, I learned that it is much easier to experience God's forgiveness when it is channelled through another human being. I may have had an intellectual conviction that God had forgiven me, but I had never *experienced* this forgiveness until my brother stood before me and said, "Mark, the Lord forgives you for those things." Second, I gained much helpful wisdom from this brother on how to avoid collecting more skeletons in the future. His counsel proved immensely valuable. Third, I discovered to my surprise that many of my sins and problems were common ones, that I was not as unique in my folly as I had supposed. My friend reassured me of this, based both on his own experience and on the experience of others he had counseled. This was an embarrassingly joyful realization. It's comforting to find out that you are normal, even if it only means that you are a normal sinner!

These benefits are valuable for all Christians, especially for those who have a problem with self-condemnation. Believing in the forgiveness of God is crucial for people with this problem, and confession makes God's forgiveness immediate and experiential as nothing else can. God's mercy, which we have previously been unable to recognize, now becomes tangible to us as it is mediated through a flesh and blood brother or sister in Christ.

If this is true for one or two skeletons, how much more so if we bring them all out! This is why many have found it helpful to make a general confession early in their lives as mature Christians. In a general confession we meet with someone in order to confess all the serious wrong we have ever committed (or at least remember committing). Since most people who have a problem with self-condemnation are uneasy about past behavior, a general confession can have a tremendous healing power.

A young woman once came to me for help in the midst of great emotional turmoil. As we talked I learned that she had committed some serious wrongdoing in her past and was perpetually tormented by shame and self-condemnation. It struck me that this woman would benefit greatly from a general confession. Since she was a Roman Catholic, I thought that she might be most comfortable and uninhibited sharing with a Roman Catholic priest. I am not a Catholic myself, but one of my friends serves as a priest in a local parish, so I arranged a meeting between them for the purpose of a general confession. After the session the woman appeared on my doorstep, beaming from ear to ear. She felt as if a mountain had been removed from her shoulders—and, in fact, one had: a mountain of self-condemnation.

If you are Roman Catholic or Orthodox, you will regard confession to a priest as a sacrament; if you are Protestant, you will regard confession only as a useful practice for dealing with special problems. Regardless of one's theology, confession of wrongdoing should be seen as a helpful tool in living the Christian life, especially for those suffering from problems with self-condemnation.

Determining wrongdoing. Our brothers and sisters in Christ can also help us by providing an objective opinion about whether we have actually committed wrongdoing or whether our feeling of guilt derives instead from a temptation, a minor fault, an imperfection, or a mistake. In other words, our brothers and sisters can protect us from our tendency to be overscrupulous.

If we have a tendency to be overscrupulous (and many people who suffer from self-condemnation do have such a tendency), we cannot trust our own judgment to accurately determine wrongdoing. We will reproach ourselves bitterly for imperfections that the Lord is viewing patiently or even with a sense of humor. How can we take on the Lord's mind? The best way is to find a wise and mature Christian, explain our predicament, and ask for their judgment. If we do this often enough, our old perspective will change gradually, until we no longer need the same kind of help.

A young man once approached me for some guidance. He began by saying that he had a sexual problem, and proceeded to explain that he could not stop himself from recognizing the physical attractiveness of certain women. As a righteous Christian man he should not even notice such things as physical beauty. I waited for him to get to the serious part of his confession, but he never went a step further. This *was* the serious sexual problem he had alluded to at first! As I questioned him further, it became evident that he had a general problem with overscrupulosity. He had a blind spot in his vision that could only be corrected by the outside lens of a brother's more balanced judgment.

If we are to benefit from someone else's counsel in this area, we must make up our mind in advance to accept their judgment even if it conflicts with our own. After all, the very reason we are going to them is that we cannot trust our own judgment: we are overscrupulous and need a more objective and balanced perspective. Even so, it can be very difficult to accept another's view, despite the fact that we do not fully trust our own. We must resolve, before our brother or sister renders a judgment, to humbly take on their mind unless the judgment *seriously* conflicts with our conscience.

Two final pieces of wisdom apply to both confessing wrongdoing and seeking help in determining wrongdoing. First, we should use prudence in deciding who to go to for help. The person should be wise, experienced, mature, and righteous. We are not supposed to confess our wrongdoing to anyone and everyone, nor should we expect everyone to be able to help us overcome overscrupulosity. Second, as the heading of this section suggests, we will only receive help if we seek it. We shouldn't wait for someone to come along and drag a general confession out of us. We must take the initiative to seek the help that we need.

Being a Help

Being part of the body of Christ means both seeking help from others and being a help ourselves. The Lord wants to free us from self-condemnation through our brothers and sisters, but he also wants to use us to bring them freedom. The main way that we can help others win freedom from self-condemnation is by relating to them directly, lovingly, warmly, and generously.

Refraining from manipulation. Emotional manipulation is widespread in our society. We grow up manipulating others emotionally and being manipulated ourselves in turn. This kind of behavior is a major cause of self-condemnation. If we want to uproot self-condemnation from our lives, we must also change the pattern of personal relating that led to the problem in the first place. This means refraining from emotional manipulation and learning to be direct and loving with one another.

What is emotional manipulation? It is the attempt to control others by expressing (usually indirectly) emotional disapproval. This is accomplished primarily by withholding affection. A woman is displeased with how her husband fails to converse with her at dinner, and so she relates coldly to him afterwards, rather than working out the problem in a more direct manner. The purpose of her action is to make him feel guilty for his conduct and to motivate him to want to please her.

Like this woman, we often want to punish and to alter the behavior of others. We withhold affection in order to get our way. This form of control is especially common in families—husbands use it on their wives and wives on their husbands, parents use it on their children and children on their parents.

In addition to this form of behavior, there are also verbal ways to indirectly express emotional disapproval and induce feelings of guilt. Imagine the following telephone conversation between a father and son:

Father: Well, Paul, are you coming home for your mother's birthday?
Son: I would really like to, Dad, but I have an awful lot of studying to do. I probably won't be there.
Father: You know that your presence means a

lot to your mother, Paul.

Son: I know, Dad, but I really don't think it would be wise for me to come home this weekend.

Father: Whatever you think best. You are an adult now and able to make your own decisions. Of course, we'll be mighty lonely without you, and your mother will be terribly disappointed that you aren't here. It will be hard to celebrate, but we will make the best of it. You've got to do what you think is right. Have a good weekend, and think of us. We'll be thinking of you.

What will the son's response to this conversation be? He will probably either change his mind and go home or else spend a miserable weekend thinking about how he is wrecking his mother's birthday celebration. The father has avoided a direct confrontation over his son's plans for the weekend, opting instead for a more indirect and emotionally manipulative method of getting his way.

These patterns of relating foster problems with self-condemnation. Over a period of time they lead us to be intensely concerned about pleasing other people and winning their emotional approval. And since we can never please everyone, we always feel guilty about someone we are letting down. It doesn't help to try to root out self-condemnation in other ways if we do not work to change the patterns of relating that caused the problem in the first place.

In contrast to the manipulative approach to relationships, our approach should be one that is clear, straightforward, and direct. If we have a grievance against someone, we should either present it clearly and respectfully or else decide to forbear in love. If we decide to forbear, then we should genuinely forbear—loving the person sincerely and from the heart rather than playing the role of the persecuted martyr. We should never withhold affection in order to punish and control. When necessary we should admonish, correct, and discipline each other in a direct and straightforward manner and in the love of Christ. If we relate to one another in this way, we can undo the damage done to us through patterns of emotional manipulation, and we can help one another to live lives free of self-condemnation.

Forgiving from the heart. Another way to free one another from self-condemnation is to forgive wrongdoing generously and from the heart. Forgiveness brings liberation from self-condemnation; on the other hand, withholding forgiveness strengthens the chains of self-condemnation. Nothing binds us to self-condemnation as firmly as the knowledge that someone else also condemns us.

Earlier, we discussed an effective way to deal with wrongdoing once it has occurred. This process for gaining reconciliation with God and other human beings is an essential element in our strategy for overcoming self-condemnation. However, if this process is to help us repair relationships and prevent self-condemnation, the person who is asked for forgiveness must actually give it. We must say the words "I forgive you," and mean them from the heart. To withhold forgiveness is to allow a relationship to be ruptured and to consign a brother or sister to the bondage of selfcondemnation.

The New Testament repeatedly emphasizes that we must forgive others even as God has forgiven us: "Be kind to one another, tenderhearted, forgiving one another, as God in Christ forgave you" (Eph 4:32). The words of Jesus in the Gospels speak even more strongly about forgiveness, implying that God's forgiveness of us is conditional upon our forgiveness of one another.

> For if you forgive men their trespasses, your heavenly Father also will forgive you; but if you do not forgive men their trespasses, neither will your Father forgive your trespasses.
>
> (Mt 6:14-15)

> Judge not, and you will not be judged; condemn not, and you will not be condemned; forgive, and you will be forgiven; give, and it will be given to you; good measure, pressed down, shaken together, running over, will be put into your lap. For the measure you give will be the measure you get back. (Lk 6:37-38)

Jesus' parable in Matthew 18:23-35 provides the most vivid example of the New Testament teaching on forgiveness. He tells of a king who forgives one of his servants a huge debt—ten thousand talents (equal to several million dollars in modern American currency). This servant then proceeds to throw a fellow servant into prison for an insignificant debt of a hundred denarii (approximately ten dollars). When the king hears about this, he is justly furious.

> Then his lord summoned him and said to him, "You wicked servant! I forgave you all that debt because you besought me; and should not you have had mercy on your fellow servant, as I had mercy on you?" And in anger his lord delivered him to the jailers, till he should pay all his debt. So also my heavenly Father will do to every one of you, if you do not forgive your brother from your heart. (Mt 18:32-35)

The parallel is obvious: no trespass against us could compare to the enormity of our sin against God, which has been forgiven in Christ. If God has forgiven our million-dollar debt how can we fail to forgive our brother's ten-dollar debt.

The New Testament teaching on forgiveness is so strong that few Christians would refuse to say, "I forgive you," when asked by a repentant brother or sister. However, it's possible to say the words and take them back with the rest of one's behavior. This is a common failing among Christians. For example, Norman asks his wife, Karen, to stay off the phone so that he can receive an important call. Karen forgets and engages one of her friends in some light conversation. Norman walks into the room, sees Karen on the phone, and angrily tells her to hang up on her friend. She hangs up and asks her husband to forgive her. Norman says, "I forgive you," but then bursts into a long tirade on Karen's negligence and stomps out of the room. Norman has said the right words, but he has also contradicted them by the rest of his actions. Karen's response might reasonably be, "He said he forgives me, but I certainly don't feel very forgiven."

Jesus issues the command, "Forgive your brother from your heart" (Mt 18:35). To forgive from the heart means to genuinely release the debt, not just "in word or speech but in deed and in truth" (1 Jn 3:18). We should forgive one another in a way that actually communicates to the other person that he or she is forgiven. The father's response to the repentant prodigal son acts as a model of this forgiveness from the heart.

But while he was yet at a distance, his father saw him and had compassion, and ran and embraced him and kissed him. And the son said to him, "Father, I have sinned against heaven and before you; I am no longer worthy to be called your son." But the father said to his servants, "Bring quickly the best robe, and put it on him;

and put a ring on his hand, and shoes on his feet;
and bring the fatted calf and kill it, and let us eat
and make merry; for this my son was dead, and
is alive again; he was lost, and is found." And
they began to make merry. (Lk 15:20-24)

The father expresses clearly to his son that he is
forgiven for his wrongdoing, not only by saying,
"I forgive you," but also by embracing him,
kissing him, clothing him, and ordering a celebration in his honor. Though we need not respond
precisely in this manner each time we forgive a
repentant brother or sister, the basic principle
remains the same: we should express in our actions
what we say in our words. If we are showing grace
and mercy with our words, then our manner
should also be gracious and merciful.

A special situation arises when we are in a
position of authority and are asked for forgiveness.
Sometimes it is right for us to punish the offense
and then grant forgiveness. The punishment may
be necessary for purposes of training and discipline
or as a deterrent. For example, a father must
occasionally punish his son if he is to raise him up
in the Lord. This is clearly taught in Hebrews.

And have you forgotten the exhortation which
addresses you as sons? "My son, do not regard
lightly the discipline of the Lord, nor lose
courage when you are punished by him. For the
Lord disciplines him whom he loves, and
chastises every son whom he receives." It is for

discipline that you have to endure. God is treating you as sons; for what son is there whom his father does not discipline? If you are left without discipline, in which all have participated, then you are illegitimate children and not sons. (Heb 12:5-8)

It is not difficult to communicate forgiveness within this context, for the father's discipline is not an act of personal revenge but of training and correction; the punishment is administered in love for the sake of the child. The young boy can come away from the punishment knowing clearly that his wrongdoing has been forgiven and his relationship with his father has been restored.

If we all obeyed the Lord's command and forgave one another from the heart, we would experience a tremendous new freedom from self-condemnation. This is one of the simplest and yet one of the most important ways that we can help one another to live with a clear conscience.

Helping One Another

We discover once again how much we need each other. I can do things for you that you can't do for yourself, and you can do things for me that I can't do for myself. You can help me grow in freedom from self-condemnation by listening to me confess my wrongdoing and by helping me determine what I have really done wrong; I can help you by refraining from manipulation and by forgiving generously and freely from the heart. As in the whole Christian life, so in this area we find that God has arranged that our progress be tied to our relationships with our brothers and sisters in Christ.

EIGHT

Special Problem Areas

IN MY EXPERIENCE as a pastor I have noticed three particular areas of life in which many people encounter problems with self-condemnation: family relationships, sexuality, and time demands. If we have a special problem with self-condemnation, one or all of these areas are sure to be troublesome. Even if we don't have a problem with self-condemnation, we probably suffer frequent guilt pangs in at least one of these areas.

Since each of these areas could be the subject of an entire book this little chapter cannot possibly do them justice. Nonetheless, it's worth looking briefly at each area in order to apply the principles presented earlier. Our examination of each area will begin with an analysis of the problem. Then we will proceed to consider what we can do to overcome it.

Family Relationships

The problem. Self-condemnation sometimes seems to hover over all our family relationships. Parents feel guilty about the way they have raised their children, children feel guilty about the way they have treated their parents, husbands and wives feel guilty about the way they have related to one another. This self-condemnation can often increase rather than decrease as the years go on, the death of a relative evoking especially strong feelings of self-reproach. Let us look at each of these relationships in order to understand the roots of this problem with self-condemnation.

Many parents condemn themselves for their children's misbehavior. Parents identify with their children and experience vicarious pride in their achievements and self-reproach in their failures. The children's conduct reflects on them, on their character and their effectiveness as parents. Other people judge the parents according to how well their children have turned out. Since children often do not fulfill their parents' expectations and desires (at least in our society), most parents experience some measure of self-condemnation about how they have handled themselves as fathers and mothers.

Parental expectations and desires differ from family to family. In many families, parents want their children to succeed in a prestigious career with a substantial salary, to have an attractive spouse and some adorable and precocious little ones. Most parents place a high value on their children's physical and emotional well-being. And most of them want their children to show an ongoing gratitude through care and support.

Of course Christian parents want most of all to see their children loving God and living righteously. A father and mother's experience of self-condemnation regarding their children depends largely on the specific expectations and desires they have for them. If their children fail to fulfill the particular expectations set for them, their parents will not only reproach their children but also themselves.

I have heard two anecdotes (they happen to be Jewish) that illustrate the pride parents take in their children's achievements and also the different sets of expectations that exist. The first story focuses simply on the parental desire for career success:

> The ladies met on the Grand Concourse, Mrs. Blumenfeld carrying her groceries, Mrs. Kovarsky pushing a pram with two little boys in it. "Good morning, Mrs. Kovarsky. Such darling little boys! So how old are they?" "The doctor," said Mrs. Kovarsky, "is three, and the lawyer is two."[8]

The second story contrasts the value of a successful career with the values of ongoing gratitude, care, and support:

> Two old friends meet.
> "I haven't seen you in twenty-five years. Tell me, how is your boy Harry?"
> "Harry? *There's* a son! He's a doctor, with a

wonderful office, with patients from all over the United States!"

"Marvelous. And what about Benny?"

"Benny? A lawyer. A *big* lawyer. He takes cases all the way up to the Supreme Court!"

"My! And your third boy, Izzy?"

"Izzy's still Izzy. Still a tailor," sighed the father. "And I tell you, if not for Izzy, we'd all be starving!"[9]

What do we want most—successful children, or grateful children? The answer will significantly affect the way we feel about our children and about ourselves.

Many children also condemn themselves for the way they have related to their parents. Sometimes they feel condemned because of negative feelings they have towards their parents. They know that they are supposed to love them, yet they often feel hostile or indifferent towards them. Sometimes they feel condemned because they have been disrespectful, rebellious, and irresponsible, especially in adolescent years. At other times they feel bad because they have failed to fulfill their parents' expectations and desires for their life. Just as parents feel guilty about the way they have related to their children, so children feel guilty for the way they have related to their parents.

This reciprocal self-condemnation is also found in the husband-wife relationship. Wives feel guilty about their failings, and husbands about theirs. Because of the intensity and intimacy of family life, spouses tend to wrong each other more often than they wrong others, with greater damage often resulting. If a couple does not know how to resolve and repair wrongdoing, then tension, resentment, and self-condemnation will accumulate over time. Divorce may seem like the only solution, but it's not much of a solution. The divorce itself may lead to even deeper feelings of failure and self-reproach.

Two special factors about modern American family life increase our problems with self-condemnation. First, emotional manipulation has become the dominant form of exercising control over others in the family. I have a friend who can recall today the way he manipulated his parents by throwing temper tantrums as a child. He would often get what he wanted by making his parents feel that they were causing his unpleasant behavior. My friend acted according to a penetrating intuition: he knew intuitively that he could make his parents feel guilty and thus get his own way. His behavior was reinforced because it was successful; it helped him get what he wanted. With such emotionally manipulative behavior deeply entrenched in family life, it isn't surprising that husbands, wives, parents, and children have serious problems with self-condemnation as they think about their relationships with one another.

The second factor is the instability of the modern American family. Our family relationships lack the stability and the certainty that used to characterize them and that still characterize them in other cultures. The skyrocketing divorce rate indicates the brittle and fragile nature of the bond between husband and wife. The tremendous rate of change in all aspects of society makes it more and more difficult for parents to experience a common life and identity with their children. Instead, the gap between the generations yawns ever wider. This instability increases the chances that husbands, wives, parents, and children will fail to live together in peace and security. It makes it all the more likely that their relationships will be plagued by resentment and self-reproach.

What to do. The most significant thing we can do to overcome self-condemnation in our family relationships is to apply the principles already presented in earlier chapters. Three pieces of advice are of special importance.

1. *Live righteously.* First, we need to understand how the Lord wants us to relate to our families. Once we do, we need to follow his instruction. This means that parents should relate to children responsibly, faithfully, lovingly, and firmly; children should show their parents respect and honor; husbands and wives should serve one another in humility, forbearing and correcting one another in love. As noted before, the best way to overcome guilt feelings is to not be guilty.

2. *Repair wrongdoing.* We should repair present wrongdoing, quickly resolving conflicts that

arise and taking responsibility for our actions. We should also repair past wrongdoing by acknowledging our failure and seeking forgiveness from the offended party. One of the first things I did when I became a Christian was to go to my parents and ask their forgiveness for my disrespectful conduct over the previous ten years. This action helped to restore our relationship and alleviate feelings of guilt on both sides. We should ask forgiveness from the offended person when possible, but also ask forgiveness from God. If for some reason we cannot ask forgiveness of the family member, then we should humbly repent before the Lord and receive his forgiveness in faith.

3. *Stop emotional manipulation.* We should repent for using emotional manipulation to control others in our family, and resolve to relate more directly and straightforwardly in the future. We should also discourage others from trying to manipulate us. The best way to do this is to talk to them directly about it. We can also resist manipulation by doing the right thing, regardless of the emotional manipulation at work. If we reward others' manipulative behavior by complying with their desires, we thereby encourage them to continue being manipulative.

If we apply this teaching with diligence and faith, we will grow in our freedom from self-condemnation in our family relationships.

What else can we do to overcome problems with self-condemnation in our families? First, if you are a parent make sure you align your expectations and desires for your children with the Lord's expectations and desires. This means that you should place the highest value on your son's or daughter's personal relationship with the Lord, desiring them to live a righteous and faithful life before God. You should also want your children to relate to you with ongoing respect and gratitude. Your hopes for your children's academic, professional, and economic success should be a much lower priority. They may not choose precisely the same lifestyle that you chose, nor value all the same things that you value, but if they are loving and serving the Lord, you should be content. This will free you from much self-condemnation, and it will free them as well.

Second, surrender your children to the Lord. Many Christian parents are so concerned that their children turn out a certain way that they anxiously and possessively try to force them in the desired direction. When the children reach a certain age, this approach is destined to backfire. You cannot force children to decide for the Lord or to live a particular way of life. They are individuals in their own right, and they will have to decide for themselves. God will act directly in their lives, but you must clearly surrender them into his hands, trusting him for their welfare. This does not mean that you forsake your rightful responsibilities, but that you recognize your limitations and put your faith in God.

What about relating to our own parents? The first bit of advice is to focus on behavior rather than feelings. As we said in a previous chapter, we are not responsible for all of our feelings; they are not fully under our control. We may occasionally feel hostile or indifferent to our parents, but this is not of any great significance. The main issue is how we are actually *relating* to them. If we are relating as a faithful son or daughter, then we can rest content.

The second bit of advice is to discern what your responsibilities towards your parents are and to relate to them accordingly. We must honor, respect, and love our parents, showing gratitude towards them for their care for us, and supporting them in whatever way we can. However, we do not have to live up to all their expectations or fulfill all their desires for us. In fact, at times an adult son or daughter *must* go against parental wishes if he or she is to serve the Lord: "He who loves father or mother more than me is not worthy of me" (Mt 10:37). We must be reconciled to the fact that we cannot always please our parents, though we can always honor them. Failure to please our parents should not necessarily be cause for reproach.

We have only just skimmed over the topic of family life and self-condemnation. Much more remains to be said. However, what has been said can provide the foundation we need to struggle more effectively against self-condemnation.

Sexuality

Many Christians today are confused about the right approach to sexual behavior. On the one hand, traditional Christian norms are being rejected by the wider society. On the other hand, many Christians are overscrupulous—dominated by irrational fears and guilt feelings—in this area of their life.

The problem. The source of most feelings of self-condemnation in the sexual area can be traced to three main patterns of behavior: major wrongdoing, less major wrongdoing, and overscrupulosity. It is important to understand the difference among these patterns, because we need to respond differently to each of these behaviors.

Major wrongdoing consists of actions explicitly forbidden in scripture that exclude one from entrance into the kingdom of God (see 1 Cor 6:9-10). These include such acts of wrongdoing as adultery, incest, and fornication. Some Christians experience problems with self-condemnation because at one time they committed such acts as these, and they have never experienced forgiveness for them. Other Christians still fall into these acts of major wrongdoing occasionally or regularly, even though they know that they are seriously violating God's commands. This causes an even more violent case of self-condemnation. As our society becomes less and less restrained in its sexual conduct, it is easier for Christians to be lured into patterns of serious sin.

Less major wrongdoing in the sexual area consists of acts which scripture does not forbid on pain of death but which are clearly not in keeping with God's intention for human sexuality. The two clearest examples of this type of wrongdoing are sexual fantasy and masturbation. Once again, some Christians experience self-condemnation because they have committed this type of wrongdoing in the past, and others because of ongoing problems. In my pastoral experience I have been impressed by how many Christians struggle with sexual fantasy and masturbation and how often these difficulties produce a serious problem with self-condemnation.

Overscrupulosity, as discussed in Chapter Five, is a term which refers to the mistaken assumption that certain types of behavior are actually wrongdoing. We are overscrupulous when we relate to sexual feelings, sexual desires, and sexual temptations as wrongdoing rather than viewing them as facts of our human condition. Many Christians relate overscrupulously to the sexual area of their life, and thus experience great shame, fear, and condemnation even when they conduct themselves blamelessly.

There are other causes of problems with self-condemnation in the area of sexuality. Some people experience condemnation about sexual play they engaged in as a young child. Others experience irrational condemnation over being sexually violated as a youth, often by another family member. Still others experience condemnation as a result of being sexually violated as an adult. All of these experiences commonly give rise to deep-seated shame and self-condemnation that remain as problems in later life.

What to do. The key to dealing effectively with these difficulties is to understand the differences between the various sources of sexual self-condemnation and to approach each category in an appropriate fashion.

The way to deal with major wrongdoing is perhaps the most obvious: stop it! We should acknowledge our wrongdoing, renounce it, grieve over it, resolve never to fall into it again, and ask God to forgive us for it. If we have done this already, then we should repent for not receiving God's forgiveness in faith. God's forgiveness is extended even to those who commit serious wrongdoing, yet repent from the heart.

> Do you not know that the unrighteous will not inherit the kingdom of God? Do not be deceived; neither the immoral, nor idolaters, nor adulterers, nor sexual perverts, nor thieves, nor the greedy, nor drunkards, nor revilers, nor robbers will inherit the kingdom of God. *And such were some of you. But you were washed, you were sanctified, you were justified in the name of the Lord Jesus Christ and in the Spirit of our God.*
> (1 Cor 6:9-11)

If we have committed serious sexual sin, then we should repent, leave it in the past, and move on humbly with the Lord.

Perhaps the most important observation to make about less major sexual wrongdoing is that it differs from major sexual wrongdoing. It is still wrongdoing, and therefore should be diligently avoided and repented of. However, sexual fantasy and masturbation should not be taken as seriously as adultery or fornication. Many people who are otherwise living righteous Christian lives have an habitual problem with sexual fantasy or masturbation that they are struggling to overcome. If we fall occasionally, we need not fast for a week and walk around in sackcloth and ashes. (If we fall into adultery or fornication, such a response would not be totally unreasonable!) Instead, we should stand up, brush the mud off our clothes, seriously resolve not to fall again, and proceed on our way.

The advice for overscrupulous people is actually similar to that given to those who have committed major wrongdoing: stop it! Only here the behavior to be stopped is not the sexual act but the erroneous evaluation of this act. If we are over-scrupulous in relating to our sexuality, we should stop being so scrupulous. There's no advantage in being more rigorous in our judgment than God is, and there are many disadvantages. It never helps to disagree with God.

If we experience self-condemnation as a result of being sexually violated and abused in the past, then we need to face up to the fact that we bear no guilt in the matter. We may be psychologically damaged and in need of internal healing, but in

God's sight we are as chaste and pure as if the incident (or incidents) had never occurred. The main obstacle to receiving healing from God may be a lingering self-pity and self-hatred that needs to be put aside so that we can turn to the Lord in faith.

One final piece of advice, discussed in an earlier chapter, that applies to all of these sexual sources of condemnation is to seek help from others. If we have a problem with overscrupulosity, we should get another's judgment about whether we have committed wrongdoing. If we are guilty of less major wrongdoing, then we should confess our wrong, appropriate forgiveness, and receive counsel on how to overcome our besetting sin. If we are guilty of major wrongdoing, confession to another person will help us in our appropriation of forgiveness and our renunciation of the sin. If we have been abused in the past, sharing and praying with another can open the door to God's healing power. We need the help of others if we are to overcome self-condemnation associated with our sexuality.

Time Demands

People in our society are probably more conscious of time than any people who have ever lived. The technological marvels of modern transportation and communication systems open up possibilities for the use of our time that never existed before. However, they also place demands upon our time that were never possible before.

This brings us to our next special area of self-condemnation: time demands.

The problem.   Many of us experience self-condemnation because of our failure to meet all of the time demands placed upon us. We are pressured from every side and faced with innumerable options for the use of our time. Two types of time demands especially evoke feelings of self-condemnation: work demands and relationship demands.

Work demands are those pressures placed upon us to accomplish as much as possible as well as possible. We can experience these pressures on the job, in our church, fellowship, or prayer group, or in the home—wherever we have clear responsibilities. The pressure may be external (a demanding employer) or it may be internal (our own perfectionist standards). In addition to tension, anxiety, and strain, the consequences of living under such constant pressure can include frequent pangs of self-condemnation.

For example, Pete is an engineer for a major automobile corporation. His boss is pressing him to put in twenty hours per week overtime; his congregation wants him to serve as a church officer; his sons want him to coach their Little League baseball team; he wants to paint his living room and build some new furniture; and his wife would like to see him occasionally. Pete's wife, Marilyn, has the kids to take care of, a house to manage, and several services in the church. Not all of these demands on Pete's and Marilyn's time can be met. They have to refuse some assignments, neglect some tasks, and do others less than perfectly. As a result, Pete and Marilyn feel guilty.

Relationship demands are the pressures we feel to be attentive to people close to us or for whom we have responsibility. These demands surface in our relationships with our families, friends, and our fellow church members. Again, the pressure may be external—a relative's expectation that we write them monthly—or internal—our own conviction that we should spend every Saturday with our sons. Again, these demands are often so great that we cannot possibly meet them all. There are simply too many people to visit, write, telephone, and spend time with. Frustrated, we condemn ourselves for our failure to serve all and please all.

Work and relationship demands are not evil in themselves. In fact, most of them are probably good things, and some may even be essential. However, if your life is anything like mine, you simply cannot meet all of the good demands placed upon you—by yourself and by others. One work demand competes with another; one relationship demand conflicts with another; work demands clash with relationship demands. The pressure to do all of these good things may give you a bad case of self-condemnation, as well as an ulcer or a migraine.

What to do. In order to overcome self-condemnation that comes from unfulfilled time demands, we need to grasp two critical principles of Christian conduct. Understanding these principles can eliminate the confusion that arises between time demands and standards of righteousness.

1. *Righteousness is different from and superior to job performance*. We discussed this in Chapter Five, but the point is worth repeating. Standards of righteousness can never be violated without guilt. Standards of excellence in performance can be violated without guilt. At times they must be violated. This doesn't excuse irresponsibility or negligence (such behavior is clearly wrong). But it is true that we can be living a righteous life, fully pleasing to God, despite the fact that we haven't accomplished everything demanded of us.

2. *Righteousness is different from and superior to pleasing other people*. It is good to please other people, but doing so is not the same as living a righteous life. In fact, if we are to live righteously, we will certainly displease some people. Our failure to meet all of the demands people place on us does not thereby render us guilty. To try to please everyone all the time, besides being impossible, simply isn't the right goal for our lives. To paraphrase Abraham Lincoln's famous saying, "You can please all of the people some of the time, and some of the people all the time, but you can't please all of the people all of the time."

Understanding both of these principles can help us determine when our feelings of self-condemnation do not stem from wrongdoing and should thus be responded to in a totally different way.

Because my own life is extremely busy, I have had to learn how to cope with formidable time demands without becoming emotionally subject to them. Several bits of wisdom have been particularly helpful.

First of all, we should find out how the Lord wants us to spend our time. He won't ask us to do more than is humanly possible, that is, for a *spiritual* human being. We should ask him what he wants us to be investing in most heavily. We should resist simply responding to human demands so that we can respond, first and foremost, to God's demands. Second, we should not bite off more than we can chew. We often take on more responsibilities and assignments than we can reasonably accomplish. We must learn to say no as well as yes and to reckon with our own limitations in time and ability. Third, we should drop perfectionist standards. I have often found my own perfectionist standards preventing me from relating to a particular task the way the Lord wants me to. We need to discover not only what the Lord wants us to do, but how well he wants us to do it. Some things should be done excellently, while others deserve less care and attention. Fourth, we should learn to schedule our time and to set priorities. In our society effective time management has become almost a requirement for successful living. The more we control our time and know how it is used, the more we will be able to make decisions about how we can invest it wisely. Finally, we should be diligent and responsible in all our work: "Whatever your task, work heartily, as serving the Lord and not men" (Col 3:23).

Excessive time demands are a fact of life for most people in modern society. The intense pressures placed upon our time cause many of us to experience a special problem with self-condemnation. Nonetheless, just as the Lord can help us overcome condemnation in the areas of family life and sexuality, so we can experience his victory in this troublesome area. Even the most stubborn problem with self-condemnation can be defeated if we live according to God's grace and wisdom.

NINE

The Goodness and the Power of God

MOST PEOPLE WHO battle with self-condemnation have a distorted image of God. Often, we see him as a severe and compassionless judge, watching us attentively, eager to punish us for any infraction. Or perhaps we see him as a kind and tolerant old gentleman, willing to pardon our sin but powerless to deliver us from its hold. These images of God insult his infinite goodness, holiness, and power; they also inhibit us from living righteously and with a clear conscience. Our victory over self-condemnation will not be complete until we receive a deeper revelation of the true character of God.

The Revelation of God's Character

One of the best ways to grow in understanding God's character is to study Exodus, chapters 33 and 34, with a special focus on Exodus 34:6-7. Jewish commentators have traditionally referred to this passage as the revelation of the thirteen attributes of God's nature. If we want to deepen our knowledge of God, this is an excellent place to begin.

The chapters preceding this passage chronicle the details of God's saving actions among his people, despite their infidelity. God redeems the people of Israel from cruel bondage in Egypt by calling Moses as his servant and working signs and wonders at his hand. God divides the Red Sea for Israel to pass through, drowns Pharaoh's army, feeds his people on manna in the wilderness, and leads them safely by a pillar of fire and cloud until they come to the foot of Mount Sinai. Throughout these events the people of Israel continue to doubt, question, and murmur, making life difficult for Moses. But the Lord deals with them patiently, like a father training a young child.

At Mount Sinai the Lord does an even greater work. Here the Lord establishes a covenant with the people of Israel, calling them to be a kingdom of priests and a holy nation. The people respond with a solemn affirmation of loyalty, "All that the Lord has spoken we will do" (Ex 19:8). Here the Lord reveals his majesty and power, appearing to his people in earthquake, thunder, lightning, cloud, fire, and smoke, accompanied by the piercing and extended blast of an angelic trumpet that grows louder and louder until the people tremble with the terror of death. Here the Lord reveals his law, declaring to his people the Ten Commandments (Ex 20) and giving them through Moses the covenant code (Ex 21-23). This is followed by a covenant ratification ceremony in which Moses, Aaron, Nadab, Abihu, and seventy of the elders of Israel "beheld God, and ate and drank" (Ex 24). Finally, Moses again ascends the mountain in order to receive the tables of stone inscribed with the divine law and to receive further instructions about Israel's worship.

The Lord has revealed his goodness, his power, and his patience. Now the people of Israel give him more of an opportunity to manifest his patience. While Moses is up on the mountain receiving instructions from God about the tabernacle and its worship, the people at the foot of the mountain make a golden calf, worship it, and declare a great feast in its honor. This is the greatest sin Israel has yet committed. They have broken the covenant so recently made, proving themselves totally faithless. Moses and the Lord are both moved to fierce anger, and the life of the people is in great jeopardy. After punishing the people, Moses restrains his wrath and intercedes with God on their behalf. It is within this context that Moses asks God to reveal his glory (Ex 33:18).

The covenant has been broken—as symbolized by the first tablets of the law that Moses destroyed as he came down from the mountain and saw Israel worshipping the golden calf. Now the Lord graciously renews the covenant and assures Moses and Israel of his continued faithfulness by revealing clearly the attributes of his nature:

So Moses cut two tables of stone like the first; and he rose early in the morning and went up on Mount Sinai, as the Lord had commanded him, and took in his hand two tables of stone. And the Lord descended in the cloud and stood with him there, and proclaimed the name of the Lord. The Lord passed before him, and proclaimed, "The Lord, the Lord, a God merciful and gracious, slow to anger, and abounding in steadfast love and faithfulness, keeping steadfast love for thousands, forgiving iniquity and transgression and sin, but who will by no means clear the guilty, visiting the iniquity of the fathers upon the children and the children's children, to the third and the fourth generation." (Ex 34:4-7)

What is this God like? How can one describe his character? He is merciful (compassionate), gracious (generous and favorable), slow to anger (patient), abounding in steadfast love (committed, loyal, covenant love) and faithfulness (loyalty and truth), keeping steadfast love for thousands (of generations), forgiving generously the sin of those who repent but refusing to clear those who cling to their iniquity.

The Lord only *declares* himself to be that which he has already *shown* himself to be in his relationship with Israel. He has initiated a relationship with this people, provided for them in distress, redeemed them from bondage, given them a law and a way of life, consented to dwell among them, and forgiven them time and again as they stumbled in their weakness and sin. He has also punished those who stubbornly and maliciously rejected his reign, and he has disciplined

his faithful ones so that they might learn to walk in
holiness; nevertheless, in everything his fundamental disposition towards his people has been
one of grace, mercy, and love. In a word, he has
shown his "goodness" to Israel (Ex 33:19). He is a
God of infinite power and wisdom, but also a God
of infinite goodness.

The best commentary on Exodus 34:4-7 is
Psalm 103. This psalm proclaims both the power
with which God reigns and redeems and also the
steadfast love with which he forgives.

Bless the Lord, O my soul;
    and all that is within me, bless his holy name!
Bless the Lord, O my soul;
    and forget not all his benefits,
who forgives all your iniquity,
    who heals all your diseases,
who redeems your life from the Pit,
    who crowns you with steadfast love and
      mercy,
who satisfies you with good as long as you live
    so that your youth is renewed like the eagle's.

The Lord works vindication
    and justice for all who are oppressed.
He made known his ways to Moses,
    his acts to the people of Israel.
The Lord is merciful and gracious,
    slow to anger and abounding in steadfast
      love.
He will not always chide,
    nor will he keep his anger for ever.

He does not deal with us according to our sins,
>   nor requite us according to our iniquities.

For as the heavens are high above the earth,
>   so great is his steadfast love towards those
>   who fear him;
as far as the east is from the west,
>   so far does he remove our transgressions from
>   us.
As a father pities his children,
>   so the Lord pities those who fear him.
For he knows our frame;
>   he remembers that we are dust.

As for man, his days are like grass;
>   he flourishes like a flower of the field;
for the wind passes over it, and it is gone,
>   and its place knows it no more.
But the steadfast love of the Lord is from
>   everlasting to everlasting,
>   upon those who fear him,
>   and his righteousness to children's children,
to those who keep his covenant
>   and remember to do his commandments.

The Lord has established his throne in the
>   heavens,
>   and his kingdom rules over all.
Bless the Lord, O you his angels,
>   you mighty ones who do his word,
>   hearkening to the voice of his word!
Bless the Lord, all his hosts,
>   his ministers that do his will!

Bless the Lord, all his works,
  in all places of his dominion.
Bless the Lord, O my soul!

The great contrast between the power of God and the frailty of man is evident in this psalm. Yet this omnipotent God, who is served and praised by hosts of angels, has compassion on us whose frame is as fragile as dust and whose days are as short as the days of the grass. He chooses to forgive our sins, heal our diseases, redeem us from death, and provide for us as a loyal father. Even as he revealed his character to Moses and the people of Israel, so he reveals his power and his goodness to those who fear him. What response can we make to this? The psalmist gives us some idea: Fear him, keep his covenant, remember to do his commandments, and bless his holy name.

So what is God like? These Old Testament passages show us something of his tremendous and awesome power. They also show that he can at times discipline, chastise, and punish. But most of all, they reveal his fundamental characteristic of goodness—his favorable disposition towards those he has created and redeemed.

Christ: The Perfect Expression of God's Character

The same character that God revealed to Moses on Sinai and in his dealings with the people of Israel is shown most perfectly in the salvation wrought for us in Jesus Christ. In Christ, God the Father gives to humanity that which is most precious to him—his own Son—that the world might not languish in sin but be brought to life. The gift of Jesus Christ is the perfect expression of God's goodness and favor.

In five short verses of his letter to the Ephesians, the Apostle Paul uses four different words to describe God's goodness in bringing us to life in Christ:

> But God, who is rich in *mercy*, out of the great *love* with which he *loved* us, even when we were dead through our trespasses, made us alive together with Christ (by *grace* you have been saved), and raised us up with him, and made us sit with him in the heavenly places in Christ Jesus, that in the coming ages he might show the immeasurable riches of his *grace* in *kindness* towards us in Christ Jesus. For by *grace* you have been saved through faith. (Eph 2:4-8)

God shows us in Christ the riches of his mercy, love, grace, and kindness. He does this by forgiving us our trespasses and raising us up with Christ into the heavenly places. A parallel set of verses in Colossians focuses especially on Christ's sacrificial death:

> And you, who were dead in trespasses and the uncircumcision of your flesh, God made alive together with him, having forgiven us all our

trespasses, having canceled the bond which stood against us with its legal demands; this he set aside, nailing it to the cross. He disarmed the principalities and powers and made a public example of them, triumphing over them in him.
(Col 2:13-15)

God shows his love for us by removing the guilt of our sin in Christ's death upon the cross. The written document (composed, perhaps, by Satan) containing a full account of our sins and their due penalty was nailed to the cross in Christ and destroyed. We receive forgiveness because of Christ's sacrifice.

Our God is not capricious. His actions spring from who he is. His character was no different when he revealed himself in Christ than when he showed himself to Moses, and it is no different today than it was when Paul wrote his letters. "Jesus Christ is the same yesterday and today and for ever" (Heb 13:8). We can trust in the steadfast love of the Lord and his readiness to forgive, even as the psalmist trusted. In fact, we have greater confidence; for Jesus Christ has come, the perfect expression of the Father's love. He has borne our sin and guilt in his death upon the cross (Is 53).

Overcoming Condemnation with the Love of God

A failure to appreciate God's goodness may not lie at the root of our problems with self-condemnation, but it is sure to be at least a product of this problem. Self-condemnation and the knowledge of God's gracious character are incompatible. The presence of one will decrease or dispel the presence of the other. How can we know the full riches of God's love for us in Christ and his power as the Sovereign of the Universe and still wallow in the depths of self-pity and self-reproach?

Even if a basic misconception about the character of God is not the primary cause of our problem with self-condemnation, knowledge of God will certainly help us overcome the problem. And, like living righteously and repairing wrongdoing, knowing God is not only an important weapon to fight self-condemnation, it is a fundamental end in itself. Whether or not we have a problem with condemnation, our request should be the same as Moses': "I pray thee, show me thy glory" (Ex 33:18).

Conclusion

WE HAVE NOW come to the end of this little book. I have tried to show how it is possible for Christians today to live with a clear conscience. Let's review what has been said and draw it together in a tidy package.

First of all, the modern, secular notion of guilt is seriously deficient from a Christian perspective. This notion fails to take account of objective moral norms and individual responsibility for conduct. It views guilt as a mere feeling, produced when someone internalizes the disapproval that others have conveyed to them. In contrast, Christian teaching asserts that guilt is an objective spiritual condition that follows upon our violation of God's law. It cannot be blotted out merely by psychological therapy, as though it were only a subjective emotional disorder. True guilt can only be cleansed and removed by the blood of Jesus Christ and the forgiveness he has won for us; we can only conquer true guilt by appropriating Christ's redemption through repentance and faith.

Second, the emotional condition which many people today call "guilt" can be usefully divided into two categories: contrition and self-condemnation. Contrition is a gift from God that enables us to fully renounce wrongdoing and to live in a way that is pleasing in his sight. It is a sorrow for sin that ultimately produces change and hope. Self-condemnation, on the other hand, is an emotional disorder that leads to self-pity, discouragement, and depression. Self-condemnation is a type of self-hatred expressed in moral terms— "I am evil and worth nothing." It is a condition that afflicts and handicaps many people in our society.

Third and finally, Christians need not be subject to self-condemnation. There are many things that we can do to overcome this type of emotional problem. We can live righteously and repair wrongdoing when it occurs. We can learn to distinguish between self-condemnation and contrition, and we can repent of self-condemnation. We can lay aside overscrupulous standards of behavior, humbly seeking the Lord's standards. We can seek help from others, relate to one another in genuine Christian love, and obtain a deeper knowledge of the goodness and power of God. The Lord wants to free us from self-condemnation, and he has provided the means of liberation.

There is certainly much more of value that can be said on this topic. I have neglected many complex theological and psychological questions that are of great importance. This is because my goal here has been much more limited. I have only sought to communicate some simple concepts and to offer some practical counsel. If I have succeeded, we now understand that self-condemnation need not be an unconquerable problem for Christians. With God's wisdom, power, and love, with the help of our brothers and sisters in Christ, with faith and perseverance, we can overcome self-condemnation and live in God's presence with a clear conscience.

Notes

1. For further discussion of self-image problems, see Mark Kinzer, *The Self-Image of a Christian*, Living as a Christian (Ann Arbor, Michigan: Servant Publications, 1980).

2. A similar misunderstanding affects self-image problems in general—the failure to distinguish Christian humility from low self-esteem. See Kinzer, *The Self-Image of a Christian*.

3. Harry E. Gunn, *Manipulation by Guilt* (Waukegan, Illinois: Great Lakes Living Press, Ltd., 1978), p. 6.

4. *Ibid.*, p. 7.

5. This material is presented in more extended form in Ken Wilson, *How to Repair the Wrong You've Done*, Living as a Christian (Ann Arbor, Michigan: Servant Publications, 1982).

6. Sr. Benedicta Ward SLG, trans., *The Wisdom of the Desert Fathers* (Oxford, England: SLG Press, 1975), p. 40.

7. Self-condemnation is one type of self-image problem. The material in my earlier book, *The Self-Image of a Christian*, is thus an important supplement to the present volume. In particular, chapter six, "Overcoming Problems of Self-Image," is helpful background for overcoming self-condemnation.

8. Leo Rosten, *Joys of Yiddish* (New York: McGraw, 1968), p. 199.

9. *Ibid.*, p. 258.